Equality of Educational Opportunity and Knowledgeable Human Capital

From the Cold War and Sputnik *to the Global Economy and No Child Left Behind*

Equality of Educational Opportunity and Knowledgeable Human Capital

From the Cold War and Sputnik *to the Global Economy and No Child Left Behind*

Erwin V. Johanningmeier
University of South Florida

IAP
INFORMATION AGE PUBLISHING, INC.
Charlotte, NC • www.infoagepub.com

Library of Congress Cataloging-in-Publication Data

Johanningmeier, Erwin V.
Equality of educational opportunity and knowledgeable human capital : from the Cold War and Sputnik to the global economy and No Child Left Behind / Erwin V. Johanningmeier.
p. cm.
Includes bibliographical references.
ISBN 978-1-60752-231-7 (pbk.) – ISBN 978-1-60752-232-4 (hardcover)
1. Educational equalization–United States. 2. Education–Economic aspects–United States. 3. Human capital–United States. I. Title.
LC213.2.J6 2009
379.2'60973–dc22

2009028861

Printed and bound by CPI Group (UK) Ltd, Croydon, CR0 4YY

Contents

Preface

The origins of this book are, in many ways, to be found in the last two works I completed with my colleague from Ball State University, Theresa Richardson. In 2003, in *Race, Ethnicity, and Education: What is Taught in School* for which she served as the first author we dealt with the nation's failures and successes in its attempts to extend equality of educational opportunity to all the nation's children and youth. In 2008, in *Educational Research, the National Agenda, and Educational Reform*, for which I served as the first author, we argued that there was always a national agenda and that education researchers more often than not responded to what was on the national agenda.

Further reflection on what we accomplished in these works, what we failed to accomplish in these works, my long-held belief that after World War II public education had clearly acquired an importance for the nation and its citizens different from and greater than it earlier enjoyed, my work on how equality of educational opportunity had been defined and measured since the end of World War II, and consideration of the many contemporary claims that the nation needed successful education reform to remain competitive in the Global Economy led to the claims this work attempts to explicate. Those claims are that since the end of World War II public education has been near the top of the national agenda, that the nation's needs for highly skilled and highly educated citizens for the workplace and for its defense and the nation's need to provide equality of educational opportunity for all its children and youth are the two topics that have

Equality of Educational Opportunity and Knowledgeable Human Capital, pages ix–x

framed education discourse as an item on the national agenda. The finding of this undertaking that was somewhat surprising was that beginning in the 1980s it was becoming clear that the nation's leaders and the nation's educators were concluding that the nation's only viable choice was to provide equal quality education for all its children and youth. In the early years of the Cold War Era, there was indeed an emphasis on identifying those who came to be designated as gifted or talented and providing them with special and enriched educational opportunities. By the end of the twentieth century, it was widely recognized that the nation had to emphasize quality and equality and the definition or measure of equality of educational opportunity was different from what it was in the Cold War Era.

In completing this work, I have benefitted from criticisms and suggestions from Theresa Richardson who agreed to read and review its many drafts. Her suggestions were indeed helpful. Its shortcomings, however, belong solely to me.

Erwin V. Johanningmeier
University of South Florida
January 2009

Introduction

Public Education and the National Agenda

Recent scholarship has reported that "*A Nation at Risk* had put education on the national agenda" (McGuinn, 2006, p. 52) and that it "catapulted education near to the top of the national political agenda" (Davies, 2007, p. 5). *Equality of Educational Opportunity and Knowledgeable Human Capital* supports the arguments that passage of the Elementary and Secondary Education Act in 1965 marks the beginning of a significant and ever-growing federal role in public education characterized by a national concern with equity and that *A Nation at Risk* and the other 1980s' reports on education show the nation's increasing interest in academic achievement and standards. This work does, however, maintain that public education was achieving a place high on the national agenda at the end of World War II as the United States was entering the Cold War and fashioning the beginning of its consumer culture and creating the citizen-consumer. Education had achieved a place high on the national agenda nearly a decade before the *Brown* decision in 1954.

This work maintains that public education acquired significance as a vital part of a national agenda in conjunction with three developments. First, the prosperity of the United States after World War II contributed to a consumer dominated culture and the phenomenon of the citizen-consumer. The nation had to expand educational opportunities in response to the increased birth rate in the postwar years and in response to the in-

Equality of Educational Opportunity and Knowledgeable Human Capital, pages xi–xiv

creased qualifications that the workplace required for entry and employment. Significantly, the nation had the resources to send its children and youth to school for longer and longer periods of time. Better-educated citizens soon took better jobs and they spent paychecks buying everything from new technologies to new and bigger houses and new and bigger cars. Increased household income allowed young members of the family to attend and even complete high school and increased the chance of affording the cost of attending college. Second, by the end of World War II the globalization of the international community was underway, and the United States' position and role in the international community were clearly challenged by the Soviet Union. As the United States found itself in the Cold War, its national security required an ideological, a military, and a technological strategy. Each of these strategies ultimately depended on higher or post-secondary education, and that had lasting implications for the nation's elementary and secondary schools. The nation's engagement in the Cold War required well-educated professionals to secure intelligence and to develop effective propaganda. That engagement also required scientists, mathematicians, and engineers to develop and to maintain the technology the nation required for its defense and subsequently for the space race with the Soviet Union. Third, and perhaps most important, it was becoming increasingly clear in the Cold War Era that the nation would have to address its long history of denying civil rights to some of its citizens, especially but not exclusively, African Americans. As the Supreme Court's 1954 *Brown* decision signified, public education was the initial venue where the struggle for racial equality took place.

Since the end of World War II, the two concerns that have framed education discussions and the many attempts at education reform have been the need to extend equality of educational opportunity or equity to all the nation's children and youth without regard to their race, ethnicity, or religious convictions, gender, or position in the social class hierarchy and the nation's need for what in the 1940s and 1950s was discussed as manpower and what in this work is identified as the nation's need for knowledgeable human capital. These two issues were directly related to the nation's desire to win the Cold War and subsequently, and certainly by the early 1980s, directly related to the nation's desire to compete successfully in the Global Economy. By the 1980s, it was clear that virtually all of the nation's concerns were related to educational equity. As Henry M. Levin (1982) explained:

> National goals of economic growth and full employment require that all citizens have the skills and capabilities to make a productive contribution to the economy. Cultural and scientific progress for the nation depend on the dis-

> covery and development of latent talent among all citizens. The promotion of democracy entails the participation of all groups in the national agenda, and this participation requires an educational system that supports such goals. Even the defense of the nation presumes that virtually all citizens can contribute to such an effort. All of these national concerns also have important implications for further equalizing educational opportunities and outcomes for groups who are handicapped or educationally disadvantaged. (p. 445)

While equality of educational opportunity has dominated education discussions and many of the attempts at education reform, it is important to note that it has had several definitions or measures since the postwar era. This work explores how the generally accepted definition or measure of equality of educational opportunity at the beginning of the twenty-first century differs from what it was in the immediate postwar era. While there have been differing definitions or measures of equality of educational opportunity, there has been a continual call from education critics and education reformers for more and better mathematics, science, and foreign language in the nation's schools.

In the Cold War Era when education was charged with preparing and producing the knowledgeable human capital the nation needed to build and to maintain its defense establishment, critics and reformers called for more and better mathematics, science, and foreign language in the nation's public schools. By the time the Cold War ended, the Global Economy had taken its place. So that the nation would have the knowledgeable human capital required for success in the Global Economy critics have called for more and better mathematics, science, and foreign language in the schools.

The concern with students' proficiency in those three subjects, especially mathematics, continues. For example, so that the nation would remain competitive, in April 2006 President George W. Bush issued Executive Order 13398 establishing the National Mathematics Advisory Panel (NMAP). In 2008, the Panel explained its purpose:

> To help keep America competitive, support American talent and creativity, encourage innovation throughout the American economy, and help State, local, territorial, and tribal governments give the Nation's children and youth the education they need to succeed, it shall be the policy of the United States to foster greater knowledge of an improved performance in mathematics among American students. (quoted in Kelly, 2008, p. 561)

The Panel's goals included recommending topics for the K–12 mathematics curriculum that were "evidence-based"; recommending how mathematics should be taught; recommending appropriate materials; recommending how mathematics teachers should be taught and supported; and, of course, recommending further research. After the Panel's report was released in March 2008, it received "commentary in the U.S. national press, including *Science*, the *New York Times*, and the *Washington Post* " as well as in several professional journals (quoted in Kelly, 2008, p. 562).

1

Public Education and the Production of Knowledgeable Human Capital

Introduction

Public education is fundamentally concerned with the relationship between the formal education—schooling—of children and youth and the production and distribution of disciplines of knowledge that are recognized as useful for the maintenance and growth of the nation politically, economically, and socially. The term "knowledgeable human capital" is explained in this chapter as a comprehensive conceptualization of relationships that go beyond the implications of the more common terms of "manpower," "human resources," or "human capital" that are mostly associated with what is required for economic production. Creating an educated population and thus developing an adequate supply of knowledgeable human capital is as much a social and a political consideration as an economic concern. Clearly, to fail to produce highly educated and highly skilled and thus highly productive workers is economically debilitating. However, given the nation's history and ideology, the social and the political arguments for providing

Equality of Educational Opportunity and Knowledgeable Human Capital, pages 1–12

equality of educational opportunity as a moral imperative are as compelling, as well as controversial, as the economic arguments.

The attention given to public education issues—the need to extend equality of educational opportunity and the need for the production of knowledgeable human capital—that have been at the center of education discourse since the 1940s have continued into the twenty-first century. From time to time, one or the other of these two issues has held center stage, but each has been at or near the top of the national agenda since the end of World War II.

Public Education and the National Agenda

As the United States was entering the Cold War,[1] public education supplied the "basic premises" for considerations of "the relation of the United States to other nations, the structure of American society, and blueprints for future domestic and foreign policy" (Conant, 1948, p. 1). Public education was then placed high on the national agenda, remained there throughout the twentieth century, and is still there in the early twenty-first century. The two issues that have framed education discourse on the national agenda since the mid-1940s are the need to extend equality of educational opportunity to all the nation's children and youth without regard to their race, ethnicity, their religious convictions, gender, or their position in the social class hierarchy and what in the 1940s and 1950s was expressed as the need for manpower. As James Bryant Conant observed in 1948, "as a nation we are indeed a long, long way from anything like equality of educational opportunity" (p. 41). He then argued "that it is obvious that the best minds of the country should be devoted to a study of the many problems arising as a consequence of our endeavors through industry and education to keep this nation prosperous, strong, and democratic" and that there was a tendency to overlook "to what extent education underlies our whole economy" (pp. 35, 38).

In this work what was earlier discussed as manpower, human resources, or human capital is expressed as knowledgeable human capital. Some may find the expression, "knowledgeable human capital," awkward, but "knowledgeable" is important and should not be overlooked. In the twenty-first century the concern is not with people who are able and willing to work but with the skills and the knowledge prospective workers have acquired. Early in the postwar years, it became clear that the nation needed not just a supply of able, willing, and compliant workers but needed highly educated workers. Since then, the need has increased significantly. Now, "Economic leaders and education scholars are calling for an increase in initiative, self-regulation, critical thinking, and lifelong learning skills among young people to meet the needs of the growing knowledge economy." To be successful in the knowledge economy students not only need to master the traditional subjects—reading, writing, and mathematics—but also need to develop "technological savvy and self-direction" (Bell-Rose & Payzant, 2008, p. 24).

The measure of a nation's human capital consists of the skills, knowledge, and abilities that its people have acquired through state-supported education. Individuals who invest in their own education can expect a return on their investment, but the nation cannot afford to rely on individual investments because "significant portions of the population lack the savings to afford extensive human capital investments" (Salamon, 1991, p. 5). Consequently, the public has an interest in the quality and the productivity of public education, and that interest entails an interest in equality of educational opportunity. Once it is recognized that the public has an interest in the quality and productivity of public education, expenditures for public education are moved from the consumption side of the ledger to the investment side.

In the Post-World-II Era there was a growing recognition among the nation's leaders that the nation had entered an era that required more knowledgeable human capital than ever before (see, e.g., Educational Policies Commission, 1956; National Manpower Council, 1960; Rosenberg, 1966) and that it could no longer afford to deny equality of educational opportunity to some citizens while providing it for others. Postwar developments soon convinced the nation's leaders that the quality and the productivity of public education were essential for the nation's welfare. Public education, as evidenced by the attention it received not only from national media and a variety of public sector agents (for example, foundations, foundation officials, chief executive officers of corporations, university presidents, and leaders of professional organizations) who organized, acted, spoke, and wrote on behalf of what they believed to be in the public interest but also from agents of the federal government, was fast becoming a national concern. The nation's leaders, in and out of government, then realized that public education was linked to many, if not all, of the nation's major challenges and objectives: national defense, national security, geopolitical challenges, domestic tranquility, elimination of poverty, civil rights (sometimes referred to as the race relations problem), preservation of American values in the face of totalitarian challenges, and economic recovery and development. Since then and through to the beginning of the twenty-first century, as evidenced by the purposes of the National Defense Education Act (NDEA) and the Elementary and Secondary Education Act (ESEA), and its revisions and reauthorizations, and the purpose and significance of the most recent revision of ESEA, No Child Left Behind, reports from nongovernmental agencies as well as presidential and legislative proposals, estimates of the nation's knowledgeable human capital requirements and equality of educational opportunity, now sometimes transformed into a call for educational adequacy (see, e.g., Schrag, 2003; West & Peterson, 2009), have framed the discourse about public education at the national level.

As early as the end of the 1940s, "major industrial and professional groups" were already beginning "to feel the manpower pinch, particularly with respect to highly educated persons" (Burgess & Borrowman, 1969, p. 124). As president of Columbia University, Dwight D. Eisenhower expressed concern about the nation's supply and need for manpower and appointed a group that "developed into the National Manpower Commission." For a decade it received support from the Ford Foundation (Clowse, 1981, p. 124; see also Ginsberg, 1975). By the end of the twentieth century, there was a "special premium on 'brain power' instead of 'brawn power' as the engine of economic growth" (Salamon, 1991, p. 1). The need was great in the postwar era. In the twenty-first century, as the nation strives to be competitive in the Global Economy, the need is even greater.

The Cold War, Equality of Educational Opportunity, and Knowledge

From the mid-1940s and into the early 1990s the need for knowledgeable human capital and the need to provide equality of educational opportunity were clearly tied to the nation's campaign to win the Cold War. Successful prosecution of the Cold War required the nation to attend to the demands for equality of educational opportunity as well as its need for highly educated and skilled workers and professionals. The conclusion of the Cold War did not remove public education from the national agenda, for the Cold War metamorphosed into the Global Economy. Just as the nation sought victory in the Cold War so it desires to compete successfully, if not dominate, in the Global Economy. The goal continues to be victory. Victory means development and maintenance of a political-economic system that will enable the nation to achieve and maintain a dominant position in the Global Economy. It is widely believed that the nation cannot compete successfully on the global marketplace unless it has an adequate supply of knowledgeable human capital. That is why the calls for educational reform are so often calls for higher standards, especially in mathematics, science, engineering, and foreign language and why those calls have been so often linked to the need for enhanced economic competiveness.

While equality of educational opportunity has been a constant topic in education discourse, its definition or measure has undergone significant transformations since education was paced high on the national agenda. Often overlooked is the variety of ways it has been defined and measured since the 1940s. As analytic philosophers might suggest, equality of educational opportunity needs to be unpacked, and the various ways that equality of educational opportunity have been defined or measured are elaborated in this work. It is important to note the use of "defined or measured," for nearly all constructions of equality of educational opportunity lend themselves to numerical expression. Between the 1940s and No Child Left Behind at least four definitions or measures have been employed: (1) Access or availability; (2) Inputs or resources; (3) Segregation or integration; and (4) Outputs, outcomes or achievement. Now, some seek to achieve equality of educational opportunity not by asking for access or equality of resources but by arguing for adequate resources (see, e.g., Schrag, 2003; West & Peterson, 2007).

In the 1940s and the early 1950s, the emphasis was on equal access to equally supported schools. After the *Brown* decision in 1954, the emphasis was on ending racial segregation in their nation's public schools. *Equality of Educational Opportunity* (*The Coleman Report*, 1966) emphasized segregation or integration and academic achievement. By the 1980s, there was, especially with the advantage of hindsight, a clear movement to turn away from access and resource considerations and toward reforms that called for accountability, standards, and measures of academic achievement. That movement can be seen in reforms implemented in several states in the 1980s, in *A Nation at Risk* (1983), President George H. W. Bush's *America 2000,* President William J. Clinton's Goals 2000, and Clinton's "Educational Excellence for All Children" that was an attempt to "build on the standards and accountability framework that had been outlined—but never fully fleshed out in Goals 2000" (McGuinn, 2006, p. 137). No Child Left Behind has emphasized academic achievement.

Significantly, what began with No Child Left Behind requires—specifically, disaggregation of test scores[2]—has found its way to the 2008 reauthorization of the Higher Education Act that "required all colleges to report separate, 'disaggregated' graduation rates for students who receive federal student aid and those who don't, along with employment outcomes for all students." It is expected that collection of those data will show whether colleges are successful in retaining students from low-income or disadvantaged families and whether colleges are "preparing students of all income levels for jobs" (Field, 2008, p. A32).

So that all students, especially disadvantaged students, would be able to meet the standards that states began to require in the 1980s, educational adequacy advocates have turned away from other measures and have turned their attention to what schools, teachers, and students need to enable them to satisfy the standards. They ask not for equality of resources between and between schools and school districts but for the resources needed to enable schools, students, and teachers to meet the standards states require them to meet.

Educational adequacy advocates accept that equality of educational opportunity as measured by racial integration of the nation's public schools has not been achieved and, in light of the Supreme Court's ruling in *Parents Involved v. Seattle School District* is not likely to be achieved, that resegregation of the nation's schools has occurred, and that the movement for educational equity, even if, in principle, successful will not guarantee that all students and all schools will have the resources needed to satisfy the levels of achievement they are required to meet. They also tend not to campaign for educational equity, for they are more interested in outputs—academic achievement than inputs or resources. Demonstrating that some schools may have fewer resources than others does not necessarily ensure that states will find and allocate additional resources for the underfunded schools. Moreover, equalization of resources between and among schools can be accomplished by moving resources from one school to another, taking resources from the rich and giving then to the poor, or by simply reducing the resources to the rich schools. Equity, as defined or measured as equality of resources, can be achieved easily without providing any benefit for the students and schools that most need additional resources.

The emphasis on educational adequacy is clearly different from the emphasis or campaign for educational equity. Those who advocate for educational equity call for closing the resource or funding gap between rich and poor districts. The emphasis on equity is essentially a focus on inputs while the emphasis on adequacy focuses on the minimum funds necessary for the desired level of educational achievement or output. The concern for equity as well as the concern for adequacy is a concern for funding levels. However, adequacy proponents recognize that the movement for equity has not been successful in producing equality of educational opportunity, for standard measures of school outcomes—test scores, graduation and dropout rates, and college attendance—reveal that the gap between the achievement of students from the dominant majority group and students from minority groups still exists. Equity "as measured by school funding, is often insufficient" (Schrag, 2003, p. 3). The campaign for equity has not addressed what is needed to address "the circumstances of different children—poor children, gifted children, children who speak little English, disabled children, children with learning handicaps" (p. 79). All students and all schools do not necessarily need equal resources. Some need more than others.

Educational adequacy advocates want all schools to have the resources that all students need to reach a minimum level of educational achievement. They argue that the education clauses in state constitutions commit the states to ensuring that all students reach a minimum level of educational achievement, and states are thus "required to ensure a level of spending in all districts that is adequate to obtain the required level of achievement" (Costrell, 2009, pp. 279-280). States, they argue, are required to provide for educational adequacy because the education clauses of state constitutions guarantee students access to an appropriate education. While the education clauses may not necessarily define or specify what constitutes an adequate education, states began to specify what constituted adequacy when they bought into the movement for accountability and the standards movement that "culminated in the 1989 National Education Summit convened by the first president Bush." That Summit "was the formal launching of the standards-based reform movement, which promotes excellence and equity by establishing high expectations for all students and ensuring meaningful educational opportunities, in particular for poor and minority students" (Rebell, 2008, p. 435).

Adequacy advocates argue that once the states began to specify and to require a minimum level of proficiency they were required to provide the resources necessary for all students to attain the required level of achievement. Once a state requires accountability and sets standards and requires students to demonstrate that they have met the standard, usually by earning a specified score on a standardized test, it has the obligation to provide the resources—qualified teachers, books, laboratories, and equipment—the students require to meet those standards. They argue that "if the states are making schools and students accountable," it becomes "imperative that states also provide the resources to enable them to meet the standards" (Schrag, 2003, p. 85).

Extending equality of educational opportunity often meant, and continues to mean, serving populations that were earlier either excluded from or ill-served by public education. In the postwar era, providing equality of educational opportunity to all American children and youth required ending what *Brown v. Board of Education* declared unconstitutional in 1954—the assignment of students to schools based on the race to which they had been assigned. At the beginning of the twenty-first century achieving equality of educational opportunity, according to No Child Left Behind, meant closing the achievement gap between those belonging to privileged classes and those belonging to disadvantaged classes.

Interest in equality of educational opportunity was and continues to be a social justice issue, and was sometimes discussed as the need to end what W. Lloyd Warner and his associates identified as "the American Caste System" (Warner, Havighurst, & Loeb, 1944, pp. xii, 19), and an issue the nation's adversary in the Cold War, the Soviet Union, was able to exploit for propaganda purposes. Achieving and then maintaining equality of educational opportunity became important not only because it was a matter of social justice but also because the nation would not be able to compete successfully in the Cold War unless it had an adequate supply of knowledgeable human capital. In the twenty-first century, that supply cannot be assured unless equality of educational opportunity is available to all citizens and no longer reserved for privileged dominant classes. To compete successfully in the Global Economy the nation needs those classified as minorities to be as well educated as those from the dominant class.

In the twenty-first century, those interested in extending equality of educational opportunity, especially to those traditionally either excluded from or not well served by public education, have seen their interest benefit from the nation's increasing demand for knowledgeable human capital. If the movement to close the achievement gap is successful, the nation will presumably have the knowledgeable human capital it needs and equality of educational opportunity will have been achieved.

Interest in providing equality of educational opportunity for all children and youth and in satisfying the nation's requirements for knowledgeable human capital clearly came together in 1989 at the Charlottesville Conference President George H. W. Bush held with forty-nine of the nation's state governors and in President William J. Clinton's Goals 2000. The merger was given full expression when President George W. Bush signed No Child Left Behind into law in 2002. However, it must be acknowledged that the emphasis on academic achievement that is so clear in what No Child Left Behind requires can be seen in the 1965 Elementary and Secondary Education Act, its reauthorizations, and *The Coleman Report* (1966).

The nation's need for knowledgeable human capital—what Zbigniew Brzezinski (1970) described as "the rational exploitation of social talent" (p. 11)—and the movement to extend equality of educational opportunity to all students without regard to their race, ethnicity, religious convictions, gender, or their position in the social class hierarchy dominate and explain criticisms and proposals, about public education made at the national level since the end of World War II. The nation's need for knowledgeable human capital was among the concerns that drove critics of public education in the 1940s and 1950s to charge that the nation's public schools had grown soft, had no interest in quality or intellectual rigor, had abandoned the traditional academic disciplines, were no longer promoting excellence, and were often failing to promote traditional American values. These were claims that public schools were not adequately preparing American youth for the nation's armed forces, the research laboratories that supplied them with their weaponry, or for participation in an economy that was increasingly employing science and technology to its methods of production and distribution.

Equality of educational opportunity is not now defined or measured by determining who has access to public education but is now measured by how much the achievement gap between students from the privileged classes and students from the disadvantaged classes has been reduced. Closing the achievement gap also means that equality of education opportunity will have been achieved, for race, ethnicity, or social class will no longer be a powerful predictor of one's academic achievement.

In the 1990s, it was estimated that for the next fifteen to twenty years more than eight-five percent of the "new entrants to the labor force" would come "from segments of the population that have historically had the most limited educational and economic advantages—minorities, immigrants, and women" (Salamon, 1991, p. 1). Attending to new populations—populations that were earlier either excluded from or ill served by public education—often resulted in curricular revisions or departures from traditional curricula. Those departures have been often followed by criticisms of public education and calls for reform. Historically, when a significant number of the students in the public schools are from economically and educationally disadvantaged families, the perceived needs of the students often resulted in the establishment of a curriculum that emphasized basic skills. Students assigned to such a curriculum are then often subjected to a regimen of continual standardized testing and not provided with the higher order skills required for meaningful and rewarding participation in the Global Economy.

Calls for reform more often than not have been calls for higher standards and a return to or implementation of curricula that emphasize mathematics, science, and foreign language and claims that more students need to study more mathematics, more science, and more foreign language. In the early twenty-first century, the emphasis is on STEM (Science, Technology, Engineering, and Mathematics). Students need to study and to gain proficiency in these subjects so the nation will have the knowledgeable human capital it requires to be competitive in the Global Economy.

Events, reports, and legislative actions that demonstrate that public education has been high on the national and that the federal government has acted on its interest in public education, beginning in the postwar era and continuing into the twenty-first century include: The United States Senate hearings on providing federal aid for public education in 1945; President Harry S. Truman's Commission on Higher Education (1946); the *Brown* decision in 1954; the enactment of the Cooperative Research Act (Public Law 83-531)[3] in 1954; President Dwight D. Eisenhower's White House Conference on Education in 1955; Eisenhower's Committee on Education Beyond High School in 1956; *Sputnik* in October 1957 and the National Defense Education Act (NDEA) in 1958; *The Rockefeller Panel Reports* (1958-1961); the Elementary and Secondary Education Act in 1965; the Princeton Conference on "Quality and Equality in Education" in 1966; the appearance of *Equality of Educational Opportunity* (*The Coleman Report*) in 1966 and the discussions and criticisms it generated; the Ford Foundation's *a foundation goes to school* in 1972; *A Nation at Risk* in 1983; the Carnegie Corporation's *A Nation Prepared* in 1986; President George H. W. Bush's *America 2000* in 1991; President William J. Clinton's *Goals 2000*; and the No Child Left Behind Act in 2002. These serve as significant markers that show a continuing and growing national interest in the nation's requirements for knowledgeable human capital and the need to provide equality of educational opportunity for all the nation's children and youth.

The federal government's entry into an area that, according to the Constitution, is a responsibility assigned to the states, was initially seen not so much as an intrusion as it was seen as supportive. Provision of federal support reflected a national concern with the quality of the nation's educational institutions (Sundquist, 1968, p. 216). In 1958 when the United States Congress passed the National Defense Education Act (NDEA), the federal government "asserted, more forcefully than at any time in nearly a century, a national interest in the quality of education that the states, communities, and private institutions provide [d]" (Sundquist, 1968, p. 179). In 1965, when the "the national government finally authorized aid for education on a large, and presumably a continually increasing scale," "the state of the nation's education [was] finally recognized and accepted as a matter of concern and responsibility for the nation as a whole, as distinct from its individual communities" (Sundquist, 1968, p. 156).

What may have been seen initially as support eventually required local and state authorities to surrender some of their control of the public schools, for they soon had to comply with federal guidelines and regulations designed to advance the federal government's conception of what was in the national interest. When federal aid for the nation's public schools was provided, it came not in the form of the general aid that public school officials desired but as categorical aid. That President Ronald Reagan's administration's "federalism" was designed to return control to state and local authorities was an admission that the federal government had not only admitted an interest in public education but also had acted on that interest and had effected some measure of control over the nation's public schools. The Reagan administration did not deny that education was important for the national interest but it did not want to assume responsibility as evidenced by its renaming of Title I of the Elementary and Secondary Education to Chapter I, by collapsing twenty-nine categorical grants to block grants, and by reducing support by more than $1 billion. Reagan's successors—Presidents George H. W. Bush, William J. Clinton, and George W. Bush—all recognized that the federal government had an interest in public education, made no attempts either to deny or to minimize that interest, and worked to have states implement the national goals they had set.

It would indeed be possible to give an account of either how the nation's need for knowledgeable human capital has developed or how the nation has addressed its need to extend equality of educational opportunity to all children and youth. At times, one or the other has been higher on the national education agenda, but neither has been off that agenda. In this work, they are not separated from one another because the claim is that they are related to each other. Each was a concern influenced by and driven by the nation's desire to prosecute the Cold War successfully and subsequently by its desire to compete successfully on the global marketplace. The nation's need for knowledgeable human capital, especially in the early years of the twenty-first century, has given preference to a definition or measure of equality of educational opportunity different from the definition that obtained in the early postwar years.

Notes

1. Bernard Baruch and Walter Lippmann introduced the term "Cold War" to Americans in 1947 to describe the continuing and growing differences between the Soviet Union and the United States. See Halliday (2001).

2. No Child Left Behind requires that students' scores be reported for racial and ethnic minorities, English-language learners, and poor and disabled students.
3. For an early discussion of this act see Hunt (1956). Hunt, then the Undersecretary of Health, Education, and Welfare explained that the cooperative program was designed to focus on three major areas: "conservation and development... of human resources," "staffing and housing [the] Nation's schools and colleges," and "expanding technology and economy" (p. 643).

2

The Affluent Society, the Cold War, and the Global Economy

Introduction

At the end of World War II, the United States turned away from the hardships of the Great Depression and the wartime economy and toward a sociopolitical economy that emphasized consumption. Unscathed by the destruction of war except for the attack on Pearl Harbor, the United States was unique in its ability to adapt its wartime economy to the production of consumer goods. It developed "a high-production, high-consumption economy" (Theobald, 1962, p. 15). Schools at all levels, but especially at the secondary and the post-secondary levels, became a significant force in transforming the lives of many Americans as they enjoyed a new found prosperity, affluence, and an improvement in their social-economic status. What was taught in schools was important not only for the required war technologies but also for economic expansion. In the early years of the Cold War, mathematics, science, engineering and foreign language became increasingly important in the nation's effort to win the Cold War. Subsequently,

Equality of Educational Opportunity and Knowledgeable Human Capital, pages 13–26

these same subjects became increasingly important as the nation sought to be competitive in the Global Economy.

From the Cold War to the Global Economy

By the end of World War II, the nation's role in the world and in the lives of its citizens was dramatically expanded and transformed. In the postwar era, the United States enjoyed unprecedented power, economically, militarily, and politically. Americans had to come to terms with a new war, the Cold War but they did not want to choose between "guns" and "butter." However, they were not required to make that choice (Hunt, 2007, p. 131), for new technologies that enabled the nation's industries to produce war materials soon produced new consumer goods in great quantities. A new mass culture—the affluent society—was created, and it nourished a social revolution that eventually erupted in the 1960s and the early 1970s when the baby boomers reached their adolescent years. Postwar youth were then urged, and eventually required, to remain in school for more years than their older siblings and their parents so they would be prepared to meet the requirements of the Cold War and to participate in the new economy. In the postwar era, even the "business man" was expected to have a college education, and that new and "increasing emphasis on the value of college training" was affecting the nation's "social structure" (Conant, 1948, p. 39).

The requirements for maintaining peace and waging war made public education more important than ever before, for they now depended on scientific and technological advancements that mostly originated in the nation's research universities. The Cold War required the nation to be prepared for the possibility of another war, and scientists and educators were essential in making the required preparations. As James Bryant Conant suggested in 1948, "If public education is as important as I believe for our success as a free people, then in the 'cold war' with the Soviet Union the scientists who assist in improving our tax-supported schools will play as significant a role as did certain physicists and chemists in the battle against the Axis powers" (Conant, 1948, pp. 36–37).

Reduced to its simplest terms the Cold War was a contest between the Soviet Union and the United States and their respective allies or "client states." Besides wanting to achieve and maintain military, political, and economic dominance over the other contestant, the objective was to dominate or "win over" those nations that comprised what was then known as the Third World, and, it must be emphasized, the Third World was mostly not white. Each contestant wanted access to the resources, natural and human, of the Third World. There were distinct strategies employed in the campaign to win the contest: military, economic, and public relations. Each strategy ultimately either involved or relied on public education.

Military. To defeat or to contain the other Cold-War contestant it was, so it was believed, necessary to have a robust arsenal and the ability to deliver large quantities of ordinance from that arsenal to the other side. Eventually, this evolved into the strategy known as mutually assured destruction (MAD). World War II and postwar scientific and technological developments provided weapons that were more powerful than those that appeared during and after World War I. The knowledgeable human capital needed to prosecute World War II and then the Cold War was significantly different from and greater than what was required for World War I. As Conant (1959b) reported:

> World War II, unlike World War I, called for more than courageous youth with a general education. There was a demand for technical specialists of all sorts. Most of the specialists needed mathematical training. The number of able males with particular aptitudes and skills suddenly became a matter of national interest. After the war, this interest never died. On the contrary, it was heightened, as more and more Americans came to realize we were in a cold war in a highly technical age. (pp. 17–18)

Even before the attack on Pearl Harbor (December 7, 1941) some 1,700 physicists were employed in defense work. They comprised not only about a quarter of the nation's physicists but also "more than three quarters of its eminent leadership" (Kevles, 1978, p. 320). The need for physicists was so great that "the War and Navy departments, the U. S. Office of Education, state [school] superintendents, and even local American Legion posts propagandized for better high-school courses and more students in physics" (Kevles, 1978, p. 320). The Westinghouse Corporation began a search for scientific talent and offered twenty scholarships a year to high school students who showed ability in science. Draft exemptions were sought for young scientists. Some even recommended that the federal government pay the expenses of students majoring in science. In late 1943 and early 1944, when preparations for D-Day—the invasion of the Normandy beaches in France—were underway and when the U. S. Army was 200,000 men short of its needed strength, Vannevar Bush, head of the Office of Scientific Research and Development (OSRD), campaigned strenuously and successfully to ensure that his Reserved List of 7,500 key scientists would be protected from the draft.

During World War II, American scientists made significant contributions to the nation's defense and security. Scientists were no longer "mere consultants." They were "full and responsible partners for the first time in the conduct of the war." As Vannevar Bush (1949) reported:

> We had, during the war, approximately thirty thousand men engaged in the innumerable teams of scientists and engineers who were working on new weapons and new medicine. We gathered the best team of hard-working and devoted men ever brought together... for such a task. We spent half a billion dollars. Congress gave us appropriations in lump sums and trusted us to decide on what projects to spend the money. (p. 6)

The scientists' university laboratories became centers for research and development for military weaponry and technology, and the knowledge industry was created. As Clark Kerr (1963) later observed, "intellect" became "an instrument of national purpose" (p. 214).

At the Massachusetts Institute of Technology, a group of scientists was assembled to perfect radar. At Johns Hopkins University, scientists worked on development of the proximity fuse. At the California Institute of Technology, scientists worked on development of solid fuel rockets. During World War II, the transition from atomic to nuclear physics was completed. Scientists had demonstrated that atomic energy could be released controlled, and used for military and possibly peaceful domestic purposes. On December 2, 1942, just a few days short of a year after the Japanese attack on Pearl Harbor, Enrico Fermi and his colleagues built and successfully tested an atomic pile at the Metallurgical Laboratory at the University of Chicago. The amount of energy the pile produced—one-half watt—was not great, but the achievement was. Fermi demonstrated that scientists could release and control the energy contained in the nucleus of the atom. At the University of California at Berkeley, E. O. Lawrence converted his cyclotron to a large mass spectrograph for the magnetic separation of U-235 from U-238.

By the end of World War II and the beginning of the Cold War, it was clear that design, development, maintenance, and the ability to deliver ordinance to the other contestant required highly trained scientists and technicians. "By V-J Day," according to Daniel Kevles, "from Africa to Southeast Asia and on to the Aleutians, civilian scientists were in vogue as strategic and operational advisers to a degree without precedent in the annals of American military history" (Kevles, 1978, p. 320). The end of World War II did not curtail the need for scientists. Rather, it was to be the beginning of the production of new scientists and replacements for those lost during the war. The war effort not only relied on the contributions of scientists but also diminished the nation's scientific capability. The war had denied the nation

150,000 first-degree scientists and nearly 17,000 scientists with advanced degrees. In 1945 Vannevar Bush predicted that by 1953 the nation would have 2,000 fewer Ph.D. physicists than were needed (Kevles, 1978, p. 341). If there were another war, so it was believed, there would not be sufficient time to assemble and train the required scientists.

Postwar defense and the strength of the nation's economy required continual contributions from the scientific community. The federal government became not only the major source of support for scientific research but also was developing an interest in the conditions and the needs of public education and how well public schools (Kindergarten through grade 12) were identifying and preparing future scientists and engineers. As was acknowledged at President Dwight D. Eisenhower's 1955 White House Conference on Education, the nation had entered a period of "international stress" that created "unusual demands for good scientists and engineers" (Committee for the White House Conference on Education, 1956, p. 12).

The National Science Foundation. Even before the war ended, it was recognized that the federal government's interest in and need for scientific research would not end with the war's end. In 1944, President Franklin D. Roosevelt requested Vannevar Bush, director of the Office of Scientific Research and Development to submit recommendations on how the federal government should support science after the war's end. In his report, Bush maintained that support of science was necessary to ensure the nation's security, the strength of its economy, and the health of its people. The United States would have to support basic research and train a sufficient number of scientists to maintain the nation's defense and the strength of its economy. He recommended the establishment of an agency that would be responsible for developing plans to meet the nation's scientific needs, support "pure research," increase the number of scientists through fellowship programs, and develop programs to improve science education in the nation's public schools. In 1945, Bush drafted a bill to satisfy those needs. Senator Warren G. Magnuson, a freshman New Deal Democrat from Washington, sponsored Bush's plan for the establishment of the National Science Foundation (NSF), but his bill was not soon enacted into law.

Bush had proposed that a board of private citizens appointed by the president govern NSF. He wanted the board to serve part time and to have the power to appoint a director who would report directly to the board. A version of Magnuson's bill passed Congress and was sent to President Harry S. Truman. Truman vetoed it because he was not willing to create an agency over which the president would have no direct control. In 1950, the disagreement between Congress and the president was resolved when the Congress and the president agreed that the NSF director would be appointed by and be responsible to the president. NSF was to fund pure research but have no jurisdiction over military research. Creation of NSF was an explicit acknowledgment that the federal government had an interest in supporting scientific research and in supporting future scientists. That interest necessarily entailed an interest in the nation's public schools. Subsequently, NSF funded programs to improve science materials for the public schools and science instruction in the public schools. NSF programs were not explicitly designed to control public education. However, by supporting programs it clearly had the means to influence the public school curriculum, and it used the means at its disposal.

While Senator Magnuson's bill was being debated, Admiral Harold G. Bowen of the Office of Naval Research (ONR) was entering into contracts with universities and private industrial laboratories to conduct research for military purposes and even pure research. By August 1946, Bowen had entered into 177 contracts worth twenty-four million dollars. These contracts employed nearly two thousand scientists and an equal number of graduate students. ONR was "building cyclotrons, betatrons, signing up astronomers, chemists, physiologists, botanists, branching out into such unmilitary studies as meteors, the rare earths, and plant cells" (Kevles, 1978, p. 355).

Public Education and the Defense Establishment. What scientists investigated, how they worked, for whom they worked, and how their investigations were organized and supported were all transformed by World War II, the advent of the nuclear age, and the Cold War. American education, from the first grade to the graduate school, became part of the defense establishment and the knowledge industry. Scientists and technicians were prepared in the nation's universities, and the universities relied on the nation's public schools to begin preparing youth for careers in mathematics, science, and engineering. Public education was now directly related to what was needed for successful national defense, for the nation's success in the newly forming technetronic society, and then for the nation's ability to compete successfully in the Global Economy.

The achievements of scientists during World War II had a lasting effect on how American science was supported and on what was expected from American education. In the postwar era, university administrators soon realized that scientists would not be willing to return to the conditions and the support they had in the 1930s. At the same time, the federal government needed the universities' scientists to continue to contribute to the nation's defense. Universities entered into contracts with the Office of Naval Research, the National Science Foundation, the National Institutes of Health,

The Atomic Energy Commission, the National Aeronautics and Space Administration, the Defense Department, and other federal agencies. Government contracts supported university faculty, their graduate students, paid for equipment, and satisfied the needs and interests of the universities as well as those of the federal government. In addition, "this university-based, government-funded research and development not only created innovative tools for warfare but also stimulated the economy by spinning out new products and technologies for civilian use" (Hunt, 2007, p. 133).

By the mid 1950s, growth in university research was supported by federal contracts and grants. In 1957, it was reported that in addition to the "growing number of research contracts at universities and colleges over the last decade" awarded by the Atomic Energy Commission, the Department of Defense was then spending "about $100 million on research at colleges and universities, exclusive of an additional $100 million for the operation of large research centers managed for the Federal Government by several dozen universities." In 1956–57 Public Health Services was expected to award grants worth between $110 million and $120 million to medical schools, universities, hospitals and private laboratories with "the largest share going to universities" (President's Committee on Education Beyond the High School, 1957, p. 99).

After World War II and noticeably after the Soviet's successful launch of *Sputnik I* and then *Sputnik II* in 1957, it became increasingly clear that public education was no longer only a local concern. It was a national concern. Public education was explicitly linked to the national interest, especially defense. National leaders argued that the nation needed to identify and cultivate talented youth, those who were, in the 1940s and 1950s, labeled as "gifted." Public schools were the venue where talent was to be identified, cultivated, and transformed into knowledgeable human capital so there would be, as Thomas Jefferson earlier expressed it, "instruments useful for the public" who would be "able to guard the sacred deposit of the rights and liberties of their fellow citizens" (Jefferson, 1961, p. 84). By the end of the 1950s, the public largely accepted that there was a relationship between an effective national defense and the quality of its public schools. By the end of the 1980s, the public accepted that there was a relationship between the strength of the nation's economy and the quality of its public schools.

Economic. The economic strategy to win the Cold War entailed demonstrating to the other contestant and to the Third World that the economic system of the United States was better because it could produce more and better consumer goods for more people than its adversary. Note, for example the "kitchen debate" on July 24, 1959 at the United States Trade and Cultural Fair in Moscow's Sokolniki Park between then Vice-President Richard M. Nixon and Soviet Premier Nikita Khrushchev during which Nixon drew attention to the great variety of household appliances on display in the model home furnished with General Electric kitchen appliances. The most powerful weapon on display at the Fair may have been the Ford Thunderbird that "commanded rapt attention from Muscovites still living in communal apartments and queuing for food" (Hunt, 2007, p. 151).

Mathematics, Science, and Foreign Language. Since the end of World War II, virtually all calls for educational reform have been founded on concerns about the nation's requirements for knowledgeable human capital and have called for increased enrollments in mathematics, science, and foreign language. When the National Commission on Excellence offered the nation its report, *A Nation at Risk* (1983), it claimed the high school curricula were "homogenized, diluted and diffused to the point that they no longer have a central purpose." In the curricula smorgasbord, "the appetizers and deserts can easily be mistaken for the main course." The choices made by students in the 1960s and1970s were reminiscent of the choices and offerings that concerned Arthur E. Bestor in *The Restoration of Learning* (1956). Between 1964 and 1979, enrollment in general programs of study as opposed to either vocational or college preparatory programs increased from 12 percent to 42 percent, and at least a fourth of those programs were far from the traditional course of study. "Twenty-five percent of the credits earned by general track high school students are in physical and health education, work experience outside school, remedial English and mathematics, and personal service and development courses such as training for adulthood and marriage" (National Commission on Excellence in Education, 1983, p. 19).

In April 2007 the United States Congress was working on legislation designed to improve the nation's competitiveness in the economic arena. That legislation was aimed at "improving K–12 instruction and student achievement in mathematics and science" (Hoff & Cavanagh, 2007, p. 1). In August 2007, *The Chronicle of Higher Education* reported that Congress was about to enact legislation "calling for more spending on science education and physical-sciences research in universities." Supporters of the bill related that it was "a vital step toward improving America's global economic competiveness" (Brainard, 2007a, p. 1).

In December 2007, it was announced that The National Math and Science Initiative, a nonprofit organization supported by ExxonMobil, would grant $2.4 million to each of twelve universities, to enable them to implement the program developed by the University of Texas at Austin for recruiting and preparing mathematics and science teachers (Brainard, 2007b, pp. A8-A10). In the same issue of *The Chronicle*, Linda Darling-Hammond (2007), observed that the nation's need for mathematics and science teachers was comparable to what it was in the *Sputnik*-Era. She related that:

> When I entered elementary school in the mid-1950s, the nation was responding to Sputnik, and our shortcomings in teaching math and science to schoolchildren were of grave concern. Aggressive federal recruitment and training programs for teachers during the 1970s created a brief respite, but those programs ended in the early 1980s. Severe shortages of math and science teachers were rampant again by the 1990s and continue today. As Yogi Berra put it, we are seeing "déjà vu all over again." (p. B20)

The need, according to Darling-Hammond (1984), was sufficiently great to warrant federal investment to support the training and the retention of qualified mathematics and science teachers. As early as 1984, Darling-Hammond reported that "there is no indication that the teaching profession is attracting new mathematics and science teachers at a rate that might potentially meet the increased demand" (p. 4). The need for highly qualified and effective teachers of mathematics continues, but there is no consensus on what the qualities of an effective teacher of mathematics are. A report conducted by the National Mathematics Advisory Council indicated that more research was needed to overcome "the uncertainty about math-teaching skills" (Cavanagh, 2008, pp. 1, 5).

When it appeared that the times, or targets, for demonstrating proficiency in mathematics, reading, and science required by No Child Left Behind (NCLB) might be subject to change (see, e.g., Hoff, 2007, pp. 1, 23; Cavanagh, 2007a, pp. 1, 13), Harold Pratt, a fellow of the American Association for the Advancement of Science, offered an editorial in support of changes that would increase the attention given to science in the nation's elementary schools. He agreed that improved and effective science education is essential if the nation is to be competitive in the "global technological marketplace." He was encouraged by the attention science education had recently received, specifically, the emphasis on Advanced Placement courses and International Baccalaureate courses in the high school as well as in undergraduate and graduate science programs, but expressed concern that that emphasis, as well as NCLB's emphasis on testing elementary school students in mathematics and reading, has led to the neglect of science and other subjects in the elementary school. The plan to begin testing elementary-school students' proficiency in science in 2019–20 was, he claimed, too long to wait. Waiting that long "will never adequately contribute to the effort to increase American competiveness" (Pratt, 2007, p. 32).

The irony is that in 2007 the prospects for young Ph.D. scientists were described as "bleak." They were having difficulty finding suitable academic positions and their chances of securing a major research grant have been dropping (Monastersky, 2007, p. 1).

It is widely believed that increasing students' abilities and proficiencies in mathematics and science not only create knowledgeable human capital but also ensure that those who do so will secure a better paying job than those with lesser abilities and proficiencies. Those abilities and proficiencies, it is often assumed, enable those who have them to be good at problem solving. As James Rubillo, executive director of the National Council of Teachers of Mathematics, claimed, "The more math you have, the more exposure you have to the problem-solving you need later" (Cavanagh, 2007c, p. 22). While there is evidence to suggest that students who complete advanced mathematics courses (e.g., algebra 2) are the students most likely to secure the higher-paying jobs, it is difficult to demonstrate that the higher-paying jobs actually consistently require that workers' mathematical knowledge exceed what is taught at the ninth and tenth grade (Cavanagh, 2007c, pp. 21–22). Yet, virtually all calls for the reform of public education have called and continue to call for students to complete more mathematics and sciences' courses. Having mastered the advanced skills in mathematics and science may or may not be necessary to complete successfully certain tasks in the new economy. However, they do appear to serve as markers that allow assignment of students to occupational tracks that may or may not require competence in those subjects but are nonetheless tracks that pay well and have high status attached to them.

In the twenty-first century, the Global Economy presents the United States with new challenges as well as new opportunities. The belief that the strength of the nation's economy and its ability to compete successfully is directly related to the quantity and quality of knowledgeable human capital produced by the nation's public schools goes largely unchallenged by the public, for early in the twentieth century educators and supporters of public education successfully fashioned in the public mind a strong connection between the amount of education (usually measured by years of schooling completed and diplomas, certificates, and degrees earned) one acquired and the likelihood of successful, rewarding prestigious, and even enjoyable employment. Americans continue to believe that the public school's chief purposes are to prepare students for suitable jobs and to serve as the social mechanism for establishing a Jeffersonian meritocracy in which the most able and the most accomplished secure the best positions. The public has believed that if students remained in school and applied themselves to their studies, they would be rewarded with a good job. As was expressed at President Dwight D. Eisenhower's White House Conference on Education, "As long as good schools are available, a man is not frozen at any level of our economy, nor is his son" (The Committee, 1956, p. 4).

The American public generally believes it has an interest in and benefits from educational reform. Studies of the relationship between educational attainment and the kinds of employment one is able to secure show that the correlation between the two is not perfect but is "very strong" (Swanson, 2007, p. 15). By the end of the twentieth century, it was clear that those who had completed high school were not receiving rewards comparable to those who had earned a bachelor's degree. For example, between 1980 and 2004 earnings for young adults (ages 25–34) increased for those with at least a bachelor's degree and decreased for those who had earned a high school diploma or its equivalent. In 1980, those with a bachelor's degree or more earned 19 percent more than those who had only completed high school; in 2004 the difference between the two groups increased to 67 percent. Between 1980 and 2004 the median earnings (in 2004 constant dollars) of those with a high school diploma or its equivalent decreased by $5,200 and the median earnings of those with at least a bachelor's degree increased by $2,700 (National Center for Education Statistics, 2006, p. 54). In 2006, according to the United States Census Bureau, the average earnings of workers age eighteen and older who held a bachelor's degree was $56,788. That was 82 percent higher than the $31,071 earned by those who had only earned a high school diploma (Sevilla, 2008, p. 11A).

Public Relations. During the Cold War, public relations entailed combating propaganda from the Soviets and producing propaganda to win over the Third World. When it came to public relations, otherwise known as propaganda, the United States was at a serious disadvantage as it attempted to win over the Third World.[1] The Third World was mostly not white, and the Third World knew that the United States had earlier confined American Indians to reservations, had confined Japanese Americans to camps during World War II, and clearly had a legally sanctioned system that classified African Americans as not white and denied them full and free participation in American society, including but not only public education.

In the 1940s and into the 1970s and even beyond, any discussion of equality of educational opportunity was unavoidably a discussion of racial discrimination in the United States. As African Americans and their allies pressed their case for full and equal participation in American society in the postwar years, more often than not, their efforts were publicly and even forcefully resisted. Those efforts and the responses to those efforts escaped the notice of neither the Soviet Union that saw fit to publicize them whenever or wherever they occurred nor Third World countries that saw fit to publish accounts of such incidents in their media and to remind personnel in United States embassies and consulates that they were paying attention to how the United States was dealing with civil rights issues.[2] As then Acting Secretary of State Dean Acheson communicated in a letter to the Fair Employment Practices Committee on May 8, 1946:

> ... the existence of discrimination against minority groups in this country [the United States] has an adverse effect upon our relations with other countries. We are reminded over and over by some foreign newspapers and spokesmen that our treatment of various minorities leaves much to be desired. While sometimes these pronouncements are exaggerated and unjustified, they all too frequently point with accuracy to some form of discrimination because of race, creed, color, or national origin. Frequently we find it next to impossible to formulate a satisfactory answer to our critics in other countries; the gap between the things we stand for in principle and the facts of a particular situation may be too wide to be bridged. An atmosphere of suspicion and resentment in a country over the way a minority is being treated in the United States is a formidable obstacle to the development of mutual understanding and trust between the two countries. We will have better international relations when these reasons for suspicion and resentment have been removed.
>
> I think it is quite obvious... that the existence of discriminations against minority groups in the United States is a handicap in our relations with other countries.[3]

In 1948 James Bryant Conant warned that "racial and religious prejudice and intolerance"—how Jews and African Americans suffered discrimination and denials of opportunity—constituted "the most vulnerable spots in our armor in the nation's "competition with the Soviet philosophy (Conant, 1948, p. 66). As Mary L. Dudziak (2000) reported, "how race discrimination in the United States would affect Cold War alignments" was an important issue "since the late 1940s" (p. 153).

That the Voice of America began broadcasting news of the 1954 *Brown* decision[4] only fifteen minutes after Chief Justice Earl Warren read the decision is significant. The Voice of America was sending the message in thirty-four languages to the Third World and to countries under Soviet control and influence that democracy worked (Borstelmann, 2001, p. 94). The nation's adversaries, some incorrectly believed, could no longer use the race relation's problem in the United States for propaganda purposes, for progress was being made. Students in schools in the United States would no longer be racially segregated, and, presumably equality of educational opportunity was to be extended to African American children and youth. That serious attempts at ending racial segregation in the nation's public schools that constituted a major source of the inequality were almost two decades away was then not known. However, Conant had earlier suggested that the elimination of discrimination and prejudice against minority and cultural groups—African Americans, Japanese, Jews, and Mexicans—was a goal that was not necessarily "attainable within a lifetime" (Conant, 1948, p. 66).

Even after *Brown*, racial discrimination continued to be a Cold War consideration. In 1957, President Eisenhower's Committee on Education Beyond the High School urged the nation not to ignore "the dramatic strides being taken by the Soviet Union in post-high school education, particularly in the development of scientists, engineers and technicians" and urged Americans to work at removing barriers based on "race, creed, origin or sex" that denied American youth educational opportunities" (The President's Committee, 1957, pp. 1, 8). As Secretary of State Dean Rusk testified to the Senate's Commerce Committee when it was considering President John F. Kennedy's 1963 Civil Rights Bill, postwar decolonization of countries, many of which were on the African continent, earlier colonized by European nations, was an "epochal development" that could not be ignored. He told the Committee that: "The vast majority of these newly independent peoples are nonwhite, and they are determined to eradicate every vestige of the notion that the white race is superior or entitled to special privileges of race." He further testified that: "In their efforts to enhance their influence among nonwhite peoples and to alienate them from us, the Communists clearly regard racial discrimination in the United States as one of their most valuable assets" (quoted in Dudziak, 2000, p. 185).

Early in 1961, Roy Wilkins and Arnold Aaronson of the NAACP told President John F. Kennedy that if progress on civil rights was not made, the nation would not be able "to achieve full utilization of our manpower resources so indispensable to accelerated economic growth." They further observed, with considerable accuracy, that: "The world-wide movement of colored people for emancipation and self-determination has given a momentum to the civil rights cause in our own country—a momentum that will accelerate rapidly in the months and years ahead" (quoted in Dudziak, 2000, pp, 156–157). When President Kennedy appeared before a joint session of Congress to ask for support for his civil rights bill, he argued that failure to act would retard "our Nation's economic and social progress" and weaken "the respect with which the rest of the world regards us" (quoted in Dudziak, 2000, p. 180). After President Lyndon B. Johnson signed the 1964 Civil Rights Act, congratulatory messages were received from the presidents of India, the Republic of Guinea, Niger, and other leaders of Third World nations. Uganda's Prime Minister Obote was "overjoyed" and related that the signing would remove "[the] basis for criticism of [the] US which communists have used among Africans with telling effect" (quoted in Dudziak, 2000, pp. 212–213).

Notes

1. "Third World" as a phrase appears to have originated in 1955 at a conference in Bandung, Indonesia. It was used to refer to those nations aligned with neither the Soviet Union nor the United States in the Cold War. The unaligned nations mostly nations populated by non-Europeans. See Borstelman (2001, p. 274).
2. For a thorough account of the attention the Soviet Union and Third World countries gave to the race relations problem in the United States see Dudziak (2000).
3. Quoted in Lawson (2004). *To Secure These Rights* first appeared in 1947. It was a response to President Truman's Executive Order 9808, establishing the President's Committee on Civil Rights, issued on December 5, 1946.
4. The *Brown* decision is, in fact, the name that has been assigned to five school-segregation cases that were first argued before the Supreme Court in 1952. Four of the cases were filed and argued by the Legal Defense Fund: *Oliver Brown, et al. v. Board of Education of Topeka, Shawnee County Kansas, et al*; *Harry Briggs, Jr. et al. v. R. W. Elliott, et al.* (the South Carolina Case); *Dorothy E. Davis, et. al. v. County School Board of Prince Edward County, Virginia, et al.*; and *Francis B. Gebhart, et al. v. Ethel Louise Belton, et al.* (the Delaware case). The fifth case, *Spotswood Thomas Bolling, et al. v. C. Melvin Sharpe, et al.* (the District of Columbia case) was argued by James M. Nabrit, Jr.

3

Postwar Expansion of Public Education and Postwar Education Critics

Introduction

In the postwar era, the public school, especially the high school, was characterized by course offerings, purposes, and students very different from those that obtained before the Great Depression of the 1930s. The new students, many first-generation students, and the new purposes schools adopted to serve the new students, generated considerable discussion and criticism. Public education not only had its traditional "friends" but also acquired, according to some observers, new "enemies." What came to be known as the "Great Debate" focused on what either "friends" or "enemies" wanted the public school curriculum to include and for whom the curriculum should be constructed. The high school was approaching the point where nearly all youth of high school age were enrolled. All did not agree that all students belonged in school; yet, the students were all but required to attend high school, for a high school diploma was increasingly required for entry into the workplace in the postwar era.

Equality of Educational Opportunity and Knowledgeable Human Capital, pages 27–46

The Postwar High School

Postwar military and economic developments clearly required an increased supply of knowledgeable human capital. Public education, especially the high school, acquired importance it did not previously have. Its increased importance was complicated by the transformation of the American high school that began during the Great Depression. Postwar youth, unlike their parents or even their older siblings, had little choice but to attend high school. As Morris Janowitz observed, before the Great Depression, "the socialization of youngsters from European immigrant families and of migrants from rural areas was in good measure accomplished through work experiences—part time and full time." However, "the transformation and organization of the labor market under advanced industrialization restricted opportunities for youth and assigned a new role to public schools." After World War II "high school graduation or its equivalent—not only in terms of social attitude, interpersonal competence, and maturity—[was] defined as a desirable and required goal, even for the lowest income groups." "Actual work requirements, changed standards of employment and trade unions, [and] new legislation about minimum wages" required public schools to "accept responsibility for all youngsters who are not college bound until they develop levels of personal maturity sufficient for them to enter the labor market" (Janowtiz, 1969, p. 9). In an earlier time students attended high school because either they or their parents believed doing so would give them an economic advantage over those who decided not to take advantage of that opportunity. Once high school attendance became compulsory, what was once opportunity was transformed into an obligation. Exercising the choice not to attend high school carried a penalty, a penalty that became increasingly costly in future years.

In 1929, just over half of high school age youth (ages 14 to 17) were enrolled in school. By 1945, two-thirds of the high school age youth were enrolled, and by 1955, it was just over 80 percent. It reached the ninety-percent mark in the early 1960s. Once virtually all were in school, it became increasingly difficult to convince students they were actually acquiring an economic advantage over their neighbors, for their neighbors were sitting beside them. Once all or nearly all have a high school diploma, the diploma ceases to be a distinguishing qualification. Not being graduated from high school became a serious impediment to success. Consequently, increased attention was given to the dropout problem in the postwar era.

Dramatically increased high school enrollments presented teachers and school officials with greater numbers of first-generation students and a new set of challenges and responsibilities. Schools were now responsible for a cohort of youth—first-generation students—who previously were not in school but on the workplace. Neither teachers nor first-generation students always knew what to expect from the other. Consequently, the social dynamics of schooling changed dramatically. Some educators were not sure they welcomed either the new students or the new dynamics.

By the mid-1950s, Hollywood produced a movie based on Evan Hunter's *The Blackboard Jungle*, and moviegoers were given a portrayal of the new school population—a population that was decidedly not middle class—and the new social dynamics. Since then, Hollywood has presented the American public with a number of movies in which the setting is in a run-down inner-city school decorated with a good amount of graffiti, populated by disinterested students who are mostly minority students, and a teaching staff—save the one obligatory hero or heroine— that is even more disinterested than the students. Such portrayals have supplied Americans with a reservoir of tacit knowledge about public schools that comes to the fore and is reinforced when critics or politicians complain about public education's shortcomings and call for educational reform, school choice, vouchers, charter schools or some other solution. Thus, it is not surprising that when surveyed by the annual Gallup-Phi Delta Kappan poll, the public grades the nation's schools a grade lower than the school their child attends. For example, in 2008 when respondents were asked to rate the school their oldest child attended, 72 percent assigned that school a grade of A or B (5 percent more than in 2007). When asked to assign a grade to the public schools in their community, 46 percent (1 percent more than in 2007) gave their schools a grade of A or B (12 percent assigned an A grade and 34 percent assigned a B grade). When asked to rate "the public schools in the nation as a whole," only 22 percent, 6 percent more in 2007, assigned the nation's schools a grade of A or B (3 percent assigned an A grade and 19 percent assigned a B grade). When asked about their impressions of Asian and European schools, Americans indicated that they believed those schools were better than the public schools in the United States. They also indicated that they believed that American students were not achieving in mathematics and science, as were the students in Asian and European schools (Bushow & Gallup, 2008, p. 12).

Some educators welcomed the expansion of public education. It was seen as a true extension of equality of educational opportunity, for the number of students who had access to secondary education was clearly increasing. However, that extension came with some unintended and unforeseen consequences. As Lawrence A. Cremin (1962) observed, "the dreams of the democratic idealists may have resided in compulsory-attendance laws, but so did the makings of the blackboard jungle" (p. 128). Enforced compulsory attendance presented educators with new challenges and problems. According to Cremin (1962):

> ... compulsory attendance marked a new era in the history of American education. The crippled, the blind, the deaf, the sick, the slow-witted, and the needy arrived in growing numbers. Thousands of recalcitrants and incorrigibles who in former times might have dropped out of school now became public charges for a minimum period. And as the school-leaving age moved progressively upward, every problem was aggravated as youngsters, became bigger, stronger, more resourceful. (pp. 127–128)

By the beginning of the postwar era, the social-economic structure of society and the social dynamics of public schooling were radically transformed, but attempts at school reform paid insufficient attention to how those transformations changed the expectations of students, their parents, and their teachers.

Youth who had earlier dropped out of school to take jobs were forced to remain in school because there was no place else for them. What had once been a population seeking and exercising opportunity became, in large measure, a captive population. That captive population lost its opportunity to be independent (students do constitute a dependent class) and often rebelled against its guardians. Eventually, some rebelled against their professors, university officials and administrators, and the "establishment." The difficulty was that there was little, if any, recognition that schools were often serving first-generation students who often were very different from those who had traditionally attended high school. The first-generation students of the 1930s and 1940s were followed by the baby boomers. A good number of the baby boomers were first-generation students but, unlike the students of the 1930s, they were nurtured and reared in the postwar affluent society and thus brought with them to school still another new set of expectations and aspirations.

In the twenty-first century if there is a relatively strong economy, "a person with just a high school diploma can probably find a job and manage to stay steadily employed." However, that person "will be eking out a living rather than truly thriving" (Swanson, 2007, p. 15). Successful completion of high school no longer affords youth the opportunity for meaningful and gainful employment that it once did; it only prepares them for post-secondary education that has become not only an all but necessary qualification for meaningful employment but has also become increasingly expensive. In addition, public schools, as efforts are made to extend equality of educational opportunity to all students, are required to serve students—students from minority groups—they have not traditionally served successfully. That reports on the nation's progress or lack thereof toward educational reform invariably report on minority students' performances on standardized tests, dropout rates, and their graduation rates that have tended to lag behind those of students from the privileged classes demonstrates that the need to extend equality of educational opportunity and the need for knowledgeable human capital have merged. Those reports also show how difficult it has been to extend equality of educational opportunity to all American children and youth, especially when the measure is academic achievement or the employment opportunities that academic achievement is claimed to provide.

Postwar Criticisms of Public Education

Whether the nation would have a sufficient supply of knowledgeable human capital was one of the concerns that drove criticisms of public education as World War II was coming to a close. Charges that those responsible for public education were not interested in excellence and had abandoned the academic disciplines and intellectual rigor were essentially claims that the nation's public schools were not adequately preparing American youth for productive roles in the nation's armed forces, the defense industries, or an economy that was employing science and technology to its industrial and commercial processes at a rate significantly higher than before World War II. At the beginning of the twenty-first century the claim is that the achievement gap must be closed so the nation will be competitive in the Global Economy.

Friends and Enemies. Years before the Soviet Union placed its *Sputniks* into earth orbits, criticism of public education was noticeable and of concern to professional educators. As early as 1948 James Bryant Conant recognized that the nation's high schools were facing criticisms and that there was a tendency "to overlook the especially gifted youth." Those who wanted "to hear eloquent evidence" about the "inadequacies" of the nation's high schools, he reported, only needed to "talk to the professors on almost any campus" (Conant, 1948, p. 65). In 1949, the Reverend Barnard I. Bell argued in *Crisis in Education* that only improved schools that focused on the cultivation of the intellect could save American culture from mediocrity and give it proper direction. In the same year, in *And Madly Teach*, Moritmer Smith warned that the nation's public schools were suppressing individuality and encouraging youth to obey the herd instinct. Unless schools emphasized the cultivation of the intellect and encouraged the development of intellectual values, the nation would soon consist of robots ready for political and economic exploitation by opponents of the American way of life.

By the early 1950s, public education was receiving increased critical attention and was high on the national agenda. Many complaints were based on the belief that "progressive education" was at the root of the problem. Some expressed concern about students' proficiency in reading, writing, and arithmetic and charged that these subjects were poorly taught. Others charged that history courses were taught with a bias that failed to present objective accounts of the nation's traditions and true values. Still others charged that socialistic or communistic views and materials had infected the schools. They called for courses that would communicate the evils of communism, the virtues of democracy, and traditional American values.

The cover of the October 16, 1950 issue of *Life*, a "special issue," warned Americans of the crisis public education then faced. To ascertain what Americans believed about their public schools, *Life* commissioned Elmo Roper to conduct a nationwide survey. Roper found "complacency and dissatisfaction." Americans felt that in general the situation was "sunny," but also indicated that the situation was "not so good as the school down the street." Roper also found some inconsistencies. For example, a vast majority—86.6%—agreed that the high school had a duty "to supply vocational training, build character, polish personality and so on." However, when asked about what they "missed most in their own high school education," three times as many respondents "wished they'd had more math, English, grammar and spelling" as those who would have liked "more vocational work" ("What U.S. thinks about its schools," 1950, p. 11). In September 1951, *McCall's* published, "Who's Trying to Ruin Our Schools," and subsequently distributed 300,000 reprints "at cost to interested persons and groups" (Scott & Hill, 1954, p. 6). In 1950, Albert Lynd charged that citizens had lost control of their schools to professional educators who had no respect for the nation's cultural heritage. The title of his book, *Quackery in the Public Schools*, left no doubt about his view on the state of public education (Lynd, 1950, pp. 37, 69).

By 1954, C. Winfield Scott and Clyde M. Hill concluded that criticisms of public education had "mushroomed to alarming proportions" (p. 3). Revelations during World War II that many men and women of draft age were educationally deficient, claims that the schools were obviously at fault, and counterclaims that the schools "deserved much credit for the success achieved by our military forces" were, they claimed, "only a harbinger of the deluge to come." To determine the amount of criticism then directed at public education, they examined the entries in the *Education Index*.

They discovered that in 1942—fifteen years before *Sputnik*—a new heading, Public Schools—*Criticism*, was introduced. That introduction, they argued, meant "that the current wave of criticism was then a large enough ripple to attract serious attention." Between 1942 and 1950, the average number of entries under the new heading was nearly eight per year. After 1950 the increases were dramatic. There were thirty-five entries in 1951, nearly three times as many as in 1950. In 1953, there were forty-nine entries, more than four times as many as there were in 1950.

In assembling their own collection of criticisms of the nation's public schools, Scott and Hill found significant complaints in the popular press: articles by Dorothy Thompson in the *Ladies Home Journal*; an article by Walter Biddle Saul, a senior partner in one of Philadelphia's prestigious law firms, in the *Saturday Evening Post*; an article by historian Henry Steele Commager in the *Reader's Digest* as well as articles in *Scientific Monthly*, *Life*, *The New Republic*, the *Rotarian*, *Time*, *Parade*, the *American Legion Magazine*, the *Saturday Review of Literature*, and several other professional and lay magazines. The amount of material they found allowed them to "conclude that both pro and con criticism must reflect to an important extent the opinions of laymen and must represent things they try to verbalize and often try to put into action in their own circles." Editors of such magazines, they concluded, certainly would not devote so much attention to criticisms of public education unless it was "good grist for their mill" (Lynd, 1950, p. 4). Such grist seems to have been just what the first wave of new postwar parents and grandparents wanted to read.

Scott and Hill warned that the sources, nature, and meaning of the many criticisms of the nation's public schools could not be ignored. The critics included "scholars and professional educators, professional writers, and outright enemies of education." Among the scholars were people who were distinguished in their fields and thus credible to the public by virtue of the important positions they held. They frequently had "given much serious thought to educational problems," but usually had "not any formal training in education." Such critics included some who "have never . . . had any type of responsible, first-hand experience, or even direct acquaintance, with public schools." They often offered "the most impressive but often grossly exaggerated criticisms." However, they could neither be dismissed nor ignored because the public was listening to them. Among the professional writers, some were "thoughtful." Others presented "insights and appreciations" that were "severely limited or debatable" (Lynd, 1950, pp. 5–6, 397–398). Some critics were "friends" of public education; some were "enemies."

Besides "friends" and "enemies" of public education, there were, according to Scott and Hill, some "who honestly do not believe in the principles of public education." They believed that education was a responsibility of their church rather than the state and sent their children to church-sponsored schools. They were usually "extremely high-minded, thoroughly good citizens" who did not deserve to be "considered enemies of public education." However, there were others who did not believe that all children could "profit by the extended opportunities for schooling optimistically provided by our public schools" (Lynd, 1950, p. 398). They maintained that ambitious attempts to provide secondary, as well as elementary, schooling for all children were wasteful and expensive. That view allowed children with special needs to be excluded from public education until 1975 when President Gerald Ford signed the Education for All Handicapped Children Act (Public Law 94-142) into law. It was then recognized that more than half of the nation's handicapped children had not been receiving "appropriate educational services which would enable them to have full equality of opportunity" and that one million handicapped children were then "excluded entirely from the public school system."[1]

Scott and Hill maintained that the many criticisms of public education could not be attributed solely to "sinister" enemies of public education, for there was "a general unrest" that revealed a concern about what was happening to the traditional American way of life. Some saw social problems and political developments they did not like and focused their attention on the schools, assuming that schools either could have prevented the problems or had caused them through some sin of either commission or omission. They believed the schools could set society back on its proper traditional course by abandoning what they believed were progressive practices and by returning to traditional practices and traditional school subjects—the academic disciplines. In the future that would come to mean implementing accountability measures, the creation and enforcement of standards, and the use of standardized tests would determine whether teachers and students were meeting the state-imposed standards. The postwar "wave of criticism" could be interpreted as "an expression of a deep-seated, abiding, faith in public education." "The fear of the schools on the part of the enemies of democracy," they reasoned, "is eloquent testimony of the faith they have in public education as the means through which our aspirations can be realized."[2]

At least "nine out of ten of the critics," as James Bryant Conant earlier observed, simply did not understand that "education is a social process" and that it was not possible "to transfer what may be sound educational practice in one situation to another only distantly related." It was not possible, to "insert a curriculum designed for one type of school, the preparatory school, into another social setting (Conant, 1948, pp. 137–138). Those critics did not recognize that there were high schools where "not more than 30 per cent of the graduates" wanted to continue their education beyond the high school. How to serve that 30 percent as well as prepare the others for effective citizenship was "a difficult question" critics were avoiding (p. 137). For Conant, it was clear that not all schools were alike or could be alike, for not all communities or neighborhoods were alike. Schools "in which 90 per cent of the children come from families who hold a union card" were quite different from those located "in a well-to-do residential suburb" (p. 85). Conant was then clearly accepting that the content of the school curricula was determined by the social class origins of the student—that there was one course of study for those who were college bound and another for those who were not.

The critics also overlooked not only how the entry of first-generation students into the high school during the Great Depression required educators to provide for a school population with an increased range of needs, interests, abilities, and aspirations but also how World War II affected the nation's schools. Male teachers left for the armed forces, and female teachers left for higher-paying work in the war industries. By the fall of 1942, the nation was dealing with a shortage of at least 75,000 teachers. In addition, "there was need for 10,000 teachers in such war-related fields as mathematics, physics, chemistry, and general science" (Waller, 1943, p. 109). World War II, like the Great Depression, transformed the high school curriculum. For example, in December 1942, the *New York Times* reported that the "content and emphasis in the curriculum" of New York City's secondary schools had been changed to satisfy war requirements. Experts from the Army and the Navy helped to rewrite the curriculum, and the schools became "armed service preparatory schools." Of the 1.3 million "prospective inductees" in school, .9 million were "enrolled in preinduction physical training," .3 million "in preinduction physics," .2 million in "vocational courses," and .5 million "in other Army-approved courses" (Waller, 1943, p. 111).

The Prosser Resolution

Scott and Hill overlooked that the public had reason to question the curricula and the practices of public education, especially those of the secondary schools. Some educators then believed that traditional secondary education, the course of study that prepared students for and made them eligible for college, was unsuitable for over half of the nation's youth. For example, the vocational educators who accepted an invitation from the United States Office of Education's Division of Vocational Education to meet in Washington, DC on June 1, 1945 gave the critics reason to question the curricula and the practices of the nation's secondary schools. At that meeting Charles M. Prosser, who had earlier served as executive secretary of the National Society for the Promotion of Industrial Education and was instrumental in the campaign that led to passage of the Smith-Hughes Act (1917), offered a summary of the views expressed by those in attendance. That summary, now known as the Prosser Resolution, maintained that:

> ... with the aid of this report in final form, the vocational school of a community will be able better to prepare 20% of the youth of secondary school age for entrance upon desirable skilled occupations; and that the high school will continue to prepare another 20% for entrance to college. We do not believe that the remaining 60% of youth of secondary school age will receive the life adjustment training they need and to which they are entitled as American citizens—unless and until the administration of public education with the assistance of the vocational education leaders formulate a similar program for this group. (Office of Education, n.d., p. 15, quoted in Ravitch, 1983, pp. 64–65)

The Prosser Resolution clearly stated that neither the traditional high school that prepared students for college, for example a high school that adhered to the recommendations of the Committee of Ten (1893), nor the vocational high school was suitable for over half the nation's youth. The majority of youth needed what came to be known as "life adjustment education" that many interpreted to mean "progressive education." "Life-adjustment education" was not, it needs to be emphasized, representative of the entire progressive tradition but was perhaps "a postwar refinement of progressive education" (Cremin, 1962, p. 333). "Life-adjustment education" was to consist of programs designed for those with little or no interest in traditional academic subjects and for those who usually came from what educators would later describe as "culturally deprived," "culturally disadvantaged," minority families, or, as Conant (1948) suggested, children from "families who hold a union card" (p. 85). To create new programs for those students, many of whom were first-generation high school students, was "to do something that would give to all American youth their educational heritage so long denied" (quoted in Ravitch, 1983, p. 65).

Supporters of the Prosser Resolution were effectively arguing for extending their construction of educational opportunity to a cohort that they believed had been denied opportunities. In this case, extending educational opportunity did not mean identical services, identical curricula, identical opportunities, and identical expectations. It did not mean granting access to the curriculum offered to the kind of students who had been attending high school. To develop programs believed to be appropriate for specific populations, usually populations that do not conform to middle class values and lifestyles, can be unfair, discriminatory, and socially inefficient, for, as was observed over half a century ago, "the high-school curriculum is a mechanism which helps perpetuate our [social] class order" (Warner et al., 1944, p. xii). Some did not then and some still do not agree that designated student populations require specially designed programs, especially, if and when, school authorities have the authority to make the designations and assignments. To select students for specific programs may produce "instruments useful for the public." It may indeed be the "rational exploitation of social talent." However, it also ensures that public education serves as an agency for social reproduction and creates the possibility that some who would be "useful instruments" will be overlooked. Failure to "rake the rubbish heap," as Thomas Jefferson suggested, is not only socially inefficient but also unjust. Failure to do so is to miss identifying those who may have the potential for adding to the pool of needed knowledgeable human capital. It also denies educational opportunity and the opportunity for social mobility to those who have the ability and interest to act on their right to take advantage of educational opportunities.

After World War II, the "rake" took the form of tests, and, according to Conant, "the development of better tests for sorting out students according to various aptitudes" became "a matter of great concern." Better tests would enable workers in the field of guidance to identify "specially gifted youth" (Conant, 1948, p. 139). However, "raking" with the inappropriate instrument—the wrong kind of intelligence test—is, as Allison Davis (1951) observed, to allow at least half the nation's ability to be overlooked and not cultivated (p. 221).

Expansion of the Common School. As the characteristics and the size of the high school population grew and grew ever more diverse, the high school lost some of its selective character. In the 1930s and into the 1940s educators emphasized that the public schools were to meet the abilities, needs, interests, and aspirations of all students no matter how diverse, great, or how limited their abilities and interests. As the characteristics of high school students changed, educators developed new conceptions of schooling, new estimates of students' abilities, needs, interests, and aspirations and defined new purposes for public education. For example, in 1936 the superintendent of schools in St. Louis reported:

> This growing enrollment in all of the secondary schools has an important social significance. Actually whether we accept it as part of our idealism or

> not, the high schools can no longer function as selective agencies for institutions of higher learning. Children who are mentally and physically capable of remaining in school are in most cases continuing their attendance beyond the elementary school age. In other words, the concept of a common school education has grown to include twelve grades instead of eight.

The revised conception of the high school required new curricula. Traditional academic offerings—courses designed to prepare students for college—were now seen as no longer appropriate for all students. In St. Louis, for example, it was observed that: "Many of the students now entering high school are not inherently academic minded." Some were slow learners; some were a "year or more retarded in mental maturity." Either the content of the curriculum had to be reduced or different courses of study had to be designed to satisfy the abilities, needs, interests, and aspirations of the new students. In St. Louis, nine curricula were offered to satisfy the interests and needs of the new students: classical, scientific, general, commercial, drawing, music, home economics, industrial arts, and something called "modified general" (Board of Education of St. Louis, 1936, p. 18). Developments in St. Louis were not unique. They were representative of a general transformation of the high school that began in the 1930s and continued into the 1940s. As David L. Angus and Jeffrey E. Mirel concluded:

> During this period, high schools shifted from institutions concerned primarily with academic and vocational preparation to institutions largely responsible for custodial care. In curricular terms this shift meant that high schools decreased their emphasis on preparing people for future adult roles and responsibilities and instead increasingly directed their attention to immediate and clearly relevant problems of youth. (1999, p. 57)

Some reacted unfavorably to bringing into school students who had been traditionally excluded and who were different from those who traditionally attended. Others feared that attention would be taken away from the production of the knowledgeable human capital the nation needed. The introduction of programs and courses of study different from what was traditionally offered to serve the abilities, needs, interests, and aspirations of a new school population—first-generation students—was not universally seen as either an extension of educational opportunity or as a progressive improvement; rather, in the postwar era, it was widely seen as a decline in standards.

President Truman's Commission on Higher Education: An Alternative View

In July 1946, President Harry S. Truman responded to a request from the American Council on Education and appointed the President's Commission on Higher Education. Between December 1947 and February 1948, less than two years after the Prosser Resolution, the Commission issued a series of reports, collectively known as *Higher Education for American Democracy*.[3] The President's Commission's conclusions, recommendations, observations, and estimates of the abilities of the nation's youth were significantly different from those implied in the Prosser Resolution. Using scores from the Army General Classification Test that had been administered to nearly ten million men during World War II and the 1942 edition of American Council on Education's Psychological Examination then used by several hundred colleges, the Commission produced a "national inventory of talent." That inventory allowed the Commission to provide the following "conservative" estimates of what American youth could achieve:

> 1. At least 49 percent of our population has the mental ability to complete 14 years of schooling with a curriculum of general and vocational studies that should lead either to gainful employment or to further study at a more advanced level.
> 2. At least 32 percent of our population has the mental ability to complete an advanced liberal or specialized professional education (*Higher Education for American Democracy*, 1947, Vol. 1, pp. 40–41).

Truman's Commission provided an estimate of the abilities of the nation's youth strikingly different from that suggested by the Prosser Resolution. The Prosser Resolution maintained that the traditional high school did not offer the school experiences over half the nation's youth needed. The Commission believed that nearly half of the nation's youth could profit from more than a high school education. A decade later (1957), President Eisenhower's Committee on Education Beyond the High School estimated "that at least 50 percent of all high school graduates could benefit from some type of formal education beyond high school, that a substantial proportion of these should be seriously encouraged to pursue a regular college program, and that many others should avail themselves of the special post-high school programs best suited to their interests and abilities" (The Presidents's Committee, 1957, p. 9).

The different estimates of the abilities of the nation's youth may be explained by what each group's focus and responsibilities were. The vocational educators who endorsed the Prosser Resolution focused on the high school, an institution that was significantly transformed by increased enrollments during the previous decade. Public school officials had been assigned responsibility for providing an appropriate education for first-generation students. Truman's Commission—thirty of the nation's educational and civic leaders chaired by George F. Zook, President of the American Council on Education—was interested in the nation's requirements for knowledgeable human capital to deal with postwar obligations and challenges. In its first volume, the Commission emphasized that the conclusion of World War II did not end the conflict between "democratic principles" and "totalitarianism" and drew attention to the perils and promises of the atomic age, reporting that "biological and chemical instruments of destruction" were then being added "to the horror of atomic weapons" (*Higher Education for Democracy*, 1947, pp. 7, 9).

Those who endorsed the Prosser Resolution were public school officials who were responsible for administering public education. During the Great Depression, they had been confronted with an ever-increasing number of first-generation students. In the 1930s there was little change in total school enrollments (K through 12). However, while elementary school enrollments declined in the 1930s because of the reduced fertility rate, high school enrollments increased rapidly, making up for the decline in elementary-school enrollment. Many young people who would ordinarily have left school at age 16 or even 14 to find jobs remained in school because jobs were indeed scarce. Employment was especially scarce for youth. As Angus and Mirel (1999) reported: "Every national survey conducted in the 1930s and early 1940s found youth unemployment substantially higher than that of all other groups" (p. 59). Those who could not secure employment often opted for schooling. In 1945, as World War II was ending and as the Prosser Resolution was endorsed, two thirds of the high-school age youth were enrolled in high school, approximately 5.6 million or 1.2 million more than in 1929.

It is not surprising that Prosser's observations and recommendations found a favorable and supportive reception. As Caroline K. Barron, principal of the Sheridan Elementary and Junior High School in Minneapolis, observed in 1951, there was a "tremendous increase in the number of young people who enter high school over the number who were in the high schools thirty years ago [the 1920s]." Schools were being "forced to concern themselves with education for the majority who do not enter college." That the high schools were "far from meeting the needs of high school youth" was demonstrated by "the studies of 'drop-outs'" and the "several millions" who were not even enrolling in high school (Barron, 1951, pp. 201–202).

While educators were responding to a new, an enlarged, and a more diverse student population, the members of Truman's Commission and Eisenhower's Committee on Education Beyond the High School were responding to how "science and invention" had transformed "the techniques of production" and required youth to possess "new skills and greater maturity" as they began their "adult roles" in society. The Commission knew that the "atomic age" had arrived and that the possible application of "atomic energy to industrial uses" would bring about "social and economic changes" that presented higher education with new challenges and responsibilities (*Higher Education for Democracy*, 1947, p. 2). The Commission recognized that between 1900 and 1940 the percent of high-school age youth (14 through 17 years) enrolled in high school had increased from 11 percent to 73 percent and that the percent of college-age youth (18 through 21 years) enrolled in college had increased from 4 percent to 16 percent. Yet, that growth, while impressive, was insufficient because "the educational attainments of the American people are still substantially below what is necessary either for effective individual living or for the welfare of our society" (p. 25). As Benjamin Fine observed in 1945, "Not how many we can keep out, but how many we can admit should be the post-war goal of America's system of higher education" (Fine, 1945, p. 96).

Truman's Commission focused on the nation's need for knowledgeable human capital in the postwar mass society. Their "conservative" estimates suggested that the needed knowledgeable human capital could be identified and effectively cultivated. A decade later President Eisenhower's Committee reported that the "demands for high quality manpower have everywhere been mounting (The President's Committee, 1957, p. 5). Not long after the appearance of *Higher Education for America* Allison Davis reported that the committee planning the 1950 White House Conference on children "emphasized that one of the major wastes of the human resources of the United States is our failure to develop at all fully the potential mental ability of the sixty per cent of our pupils who come from the lower socio-economic groups." It was necessary to identify and cultivate the ability to be found in the lower classes, for the nation's industries, business, and the Armed Services all had an urgent need for "more able people." It was necessary to "find more of the people with quick minds and native-ability in the great reservoir of the lower-income groups" so that the United States would "be able to compete with the vast populations of Western Europe or Asia" (Davis, 1951, p. 221). As recorded earlier, in the early twenty-first century, Americans believed that the public schools in the United States were not quite as good as those in Europe and Asia.

Other Critics and Criticisms

At the 1952 meeting of the American Historical Association, Arthur Bestor, professor of history at the University of Illinois, proposed that the community of scholars assume responsibility for the nation's public schools, especially the high schools. The series of resolutions he presented received the support of nearly seven hundred scholars from colleges and universities throughout the nation, and his proposals were discussed on the editorial pages of a number of newspapers. In *Educational Wastelands* (1955) Bestor charged that the schools had been taken over by professional educators who lacked respect for the academic disciplines and had no appreciation for the cultivation of the intellect. He charged that the educators were constructing an "iron curtain" across the nation, behind which were "slave-labor campuses" where educators imprisoned public-school teachers. Only the public could save the schools and free the teachers by insisting that schools be supervised not by educators who advocated narrow vocational education and life adjustment education, but by the kind of educators capable of commanding the respect of scientists, scholars, and professionals.

In *The Restoration of Learning* (1956) Bestor once again emphasized that the public school should be "a place of thorough and disciplined intellectual training" and called for "rigorous intellectual discipline." He called for a return to traditional school subjects (science, mathematics, history, English, and foreign languages), because those subjects constituted the only true foundation for "contemporary life." While he maintained that there were fundamental disciplines and that he wanted a "restoration of leaning," he acknowledged that the school's curriculum had to relate to the modern world. To understand their contemporary world, students needed not "the simple-minded conception of mathematics as primarily a matter of making change and figuring out how many cups of punch can be dipped from a gallon bowl" but algebra, trigonometry, and calculus. To understand developments encountered in their daily social and economic lives and the products they used in their daily lives, students needed to know the academic disciplines. Advanced physics would enable students to understand television, a device then found in half the nation's homes. Use of antibiotics and vitamins required knowledge of biochemistry. Use of plastics and detergents required study of chemistry (Bestor, 1956, pp. 40–41).

Bestor presented statistics to support his claim that enrollments in high school mathematics and science courses had declined significantly. Between the beginning and the middle of the twentieth century, enrollment in science courses fell from 83.9 to 53.8 percent. The decline in mathematics courses was nearly the same. The decline in enrollment in foreign language courses was even greater, from 72.2 to 21.8 percent (Bestor, 1956, pp. 42–43). Bestor did not report that a greater percent of the high school-age population was in school in the 1950s than was enrolled before the Great Depression. The focus on students' proficiency in traditional school subjects, especially mathematics, continues. For example, the National Assessment of Educational Progress (NAEP) reported that in 2005 only 23 percent of high school seniors scored at or above proficient in mathematics (Brown, 2007, p. 1).

The Committee of Ten and The Cardinal Principles. Bestor was effectively arguing for the kind of high school curricula presented by Charles W. Eliot's Committee of Ten in 1893, later recommended by James Bryant Conant after *Sputnik,* and then again by the authors of *A Nation at Risk* in 1983. Ever since the Committee of Ten, Americans have discussed their high schools either in terms established by the Committee of Ten or in terms of the seven cardinal principles established by Commission for the Reorganization of Secondary Education (CRSE) in 1918. They have argued for fewer or more required subjects, fewer or more elective subjects, for identifying and cultivating the talents of students identified as gifted or serving the interests of students not interested in or destined for college.

The Committee of Ten, it will be recalled, was charged with recommending high school curricula that would serve those students who were headed for college. Significantly, the Committee of Ten recommended against differentiating the teaching of subjects based on whether students were or were not planning to attend college, for it was believed that those school subjects that best prepared students for college also best prepared them for the tasks and problems they would face in their daily lives. However, contrary to the recommendations of the Committee of Ten, many high schools eventually developed a two-track system: one for college-bound students and one for students who were presumably "preparing for life," for a job. As that two-track system was implemented, students' social class standings and courses of study were often highly correlated. That correlation, as Warner and his associates argued, constituted a denial of equality of educational opportunity (Warner et al., 1944, p. 51). That differentiation increased in the 1930s and the 1940s as high school enrollments increased and as educators sought ways to satisfy the abilities, needs, interests, and aspirations of first-generation students.

Twenty-five years after the Committee of Ten issued its report, the Commission for the Reorganization of Secondary Education claimed that the high schools had not been serving the needs and aspirations of all the nation's youth. The CRSE saw the high school not as an institution to prepare a select few for college but as an institution that would address the interests and needs of all youth until they reached age eighteen. The CRSE did not recommend specific subjects as did the Committee of Ten but offered seven educational objectives, the Cardinal Principles: (1) Health; (2) Command of fundamental processes (reading, writing, arithmetic, and oral and written expression); (3) Worthy home-membership; (4) Vocation; (5) Citizenship; (6) Worthy use of leisure; and (7) Ethical character. According to the CRSE, "secondary education should be determined by the needs of the society to be served, the character of the individuals to be educated, and the knowledge of educational theory and practice available" (Commission on the Reorganization of Secondary Education, 1918, p. 7).

What the CRSE recommended in 1918 can be said to have been acted upon in the 1930s and 1940s when high school enrollments grew and grew more diverse. In the postwar era the critics of public education were essentially arguing against what the CRSE recommended and for a return to something like what the Committee of Ten recommended in 1893. Since then, these two conceptions of what should constitute secondary education can be seen as framing the continual discussion about the content and purposes of secondary education. When the nation is concerned about its supply of knowledgeable human capital and its ability to compete in the international arena, schools move toward what the Committee of Ten recommended. When schools have been confronted with serving populations it has either not previously served or poorly served, schools have tended to move toward what the CRSE recommended.

Soviet Schools and American Schools. By 1958, shortly after the Soviet's successful launches of *Sputnik I* and *Sputnik II,* John Gunther's *Inside Russia Today* gave Americans an opportunity to compare their public schools to those of the Soviet Union (Russia and the Soviet Union were then often and incorrectly considered being one and the same). That Gunther's title included "Russia" was a clear reference to the nation's adversary in the Cold War. Gunther neither emphasized nor discussed educational objectives but focused on the subjects students did or did not study and how much time they did or did not spend studying those subjects. Children in the United States attended school five days a week; Soviet children attended six. The Soviet school year was thirty-three days longer than the U.S.A.'s. Soviet students completed a curriculum that included ten years of mathematics, four years of chemistry, five years of physics and six years of biology. Compared with Soviet students, American children studied very little science. Only half of the American students enrolled in a one-year physics course. Almost two-thirds enrolled in chemistry, but it too was but a one-year course. Soviet students studied English; American students did not study Russian.

Gunther's account convinced many that Soviet students knew more science and mathematics than American college graduates.

Those who may have overlooked Gunther's comparison of Soviet and American schools and students had an opportunity to consider the differences if they looked at the March 24, 1958 issue of *Life* that compared the achievements and activities of a Soviet high school student to those of an American student. *Life* told Americans that their children were not studying enough mathematics and science; the Soviet Union was producing more scientists and engineers than the United States; American schools were neglecting the gifted students, and something needed to be done about the anti-intellectualism of American schools. In the twenty-first century, the emphasis has been on comparing how well American students perform in mathematics and science on the Program for International Student Assessment (PISA) to the performance of students from industrialized countries (see, e.g., Cavanagh, 2007b, pp. 1, 13).

That postwar critics were claiming that not enough students were studying mathematics and science, especially chemistry and physics, can be seen as their awareness of the kind of knowledgeable human capital the nation needed to compete successfully in the Cold War. The Cold War has ended, but the Global Economy has taken its place. Better schools are needed so Americans can be competitive on the global marketplace. Better schools are those that enroll more students in mathematics and science and graduate more students who have done well in mathematics and science. Schools that improve curricula and instruction in mathematics and science, and enroll more students in mathematics and science, are better schools.

Life had earlier reported that the "nation's educational leaders, an assortment of businessmen, military men, college presidents and foundation officials" who had been trying to get the nation to put "some muscle into its flabby educational system" were finally meeting with some success. President Eisenhower had approved a proposal by Marion B. Folsom, Secretary of Health, Education, and Welfare, to provide funds to support a nationwide talent hunt and to improve the teaching of science and mathematics in the public schools. The Eisenhower administration was finally acting on what others had earlier proposed. *Life* reported that James Bryant Conant had been proposing "better opportunities for talented students" and, as a member of the Educational Policies Commission, was among the first to draw attention to the need to have more able students study mathematics and science. The American Association for the Advancement of Science had also been urging improved science teaching in the high schools. The Carnegie Corporation of New York had been supporting programs to improve the teaching of high school mathematics, including the efforts of the University of Illinois Committee on School Mathematics (Educators, 1958, pp. 16–18).

Life later complained that gifted children were not receiving "the best education the nation can provide." A combination of "ignorance," "prejudice," and the "inflexibility" of the nation's school's were depriving approximately 20 percent of children—the gifted children—the education they deserved. That deprivation was a form of gross inefficiency, for gifted children were capable of completing twelve years of schooling in ten. Clearly, the nation needed to make appropriate provision for gifted students. Only about 5 percent of the nation's high schools had programs for the gifted. There were even fewer gifted programs at the elementary level ("How U.S. wastes its gifted children," 1958, p. 96).

Educators had no choice but to respond to the critics. They did so by turning to "excellence." Students were now expected to accomplish more and accomplish it quickly. Those who had been criticizing the schools a few years earlier earned a new respect and popularity. For example, in 1955 Rudolf Flesch's *Why Johnny Can't Read—and What You Can Do About It* received little attention. After *Sputnik* it became a best seller.

Notes

1. Public Law 94-142 reprinted in Levine and Wexler (1981, p. 192).
2. Ibid., p. 199.
3. *Higher Education for American Democracy: A Report of the President's Commission on Higher Education* (New York: Harper & Brothers, 1948) consists of six volumes: Volume I, "Establishing the Goals," issued on December 15, 1947; Volume II, "Equalizing and Expanding Individual Opportunity," issued on December 22, 1947; Volume III, "Organizing Higher Education," issued on January 12, 1948; Volume IV, "Staffing Higher Education," issued on January 26, 1948; Volume V, "Financing Higher Education," and Volume VI, "Resource Data." For a recent discussion of President Truman's Commission on Higher Education see Reuben and Perkins (2007, pp. 265–276).

4

Equality of Educational Opportunity: The Ideal and the Reality

Introduction

The history of education in the United States can be characterized by the promise of equality of educational opportunity and the failure to deliver on that promise. The promise and the failure have been conflated by the nation's history that included racial slavery, Black Codes, Jim Crow Laws, and many forms of discrimination, some very subtle and some not so subtle. In the postwar era, it was becoming increasingly clear to many of the nation's leaders that the contradictions between the nation's professed ideals and its discriminatory practices had to be addressed and resolved. In 1954, when the Supreme Court ruled in *Brown* that separate but equal was not equal in public education, there was the expectation that all American children and youth would have equal access to equally supported public schools. The *Coleman Report* (1966) revealed that what *Brown* promised, was slow in arriving.

While the failure to provide equality of educational opportunity was discussed as a political, a social, and a moral issue, it was in the postwar era,

Equality of Educational Opportunity and Knowledgeable Human Capital, pages 47–72

and especially in the 1950s and beyond, seen by the nation's leaders as the nation's failure to cultivate fairly and fully all the talent at its disposal.

Equality of Educational Opportunity: Definitions and Measures

In the early 1940s, W. Lloyd Warner and his associates argued that unrestricted access to education constituted equality of educational opportunity. They claimed, that equality of educational opportunity obtained "if all children and young people went to schools of their own choosing as long as they or their parents pleased." The subtext of their claim was that there was little or no equality of educational opportunity in the United States, for African American children in several states had no choice; they were only able to attend the racially segregated schools to which they were assigned. Significantly, one could count how many had their choice satisfied or denied. The level or degree of equality of educational opportunity that obtained in a community, city, or state could be expressed numerically.

Another measure of equality of educational opportunity was to be determined by examining the relationship between one's "intellectual ability" and the access one had to formal schooling. "For example, if all boys and girls with I.Q.'s over 100 were able to attend high school up to age eighteen, and if all young people with I.Q.'s over 110 were able to attend college for four years, we could say that equality of educational opportunity existed to a considerable degree" (Warner et al., 1944, p. 51). Because one's social-economic status—the income of one's parents—was more often than not directly related to one's high school attendance and one's college attendance, equality of educational opportunity did not exist. Studies revealed that parents' income was a good predictor of who would or would not remain in school regardless of a student's ability (pp. 52–53). If one knew a student's social-economic status, one could, with considerable confidence, assign the probability of his/her chances of attending college.

After considering what was reported in *Who Shall Be Educated?,* James Bryant Conant endorsed what Warner and his associates reported. He then argued that the discrepancy between what Americans professed about educational opportunity and the reality was "so great as to be almost shocking." According to Conant (1948):

> Anyone familiar with education knows that for a very considerable portion of the population it is the family financial status which places a ceiling on the educational ambitions of even the brilliant youth. The oft-repeated statement

> in certain smug circles that "any boy who has what it takes can get all the education he wants in the U.S.A." just is not so; it is contrary to the facts. (p. 43)

As long as there existed what Warner and his associates described as the American Caste system, African Americans were denied equality of educational opportunity, for their access to education was severely restricted (Warner et al., 1944, pp. 120–121, 124, 137), especially to graduate and professional education. Denying African Americans educational opportunities and facilities equal to those available to whites proved to be an effective way to maintain white dominance and the subordination of African Americans in a caste-like system. In the 1930s and 1940s Legal Defense Fund attorneys were able to demonstrate that in several states, opportunities for graduate education and professional education were available for whites while African Americans had little and often no access to graduate education or professional education. For example, in the 1930s two schools, Howard in Washington, D.C. and Meharry in Tennessee, were responsible for training nearly half of the African American physicians (Neckerman, 2007, p. 44). Access to graduate education and professional education was denied by those who controlled the caste-like system.[1]

Public education was claimed to be the institution that provided children with the opportunity for social mobility. However, as Conant observed after reading *Who Shall Be Educated?*, "to the extent that educational opportunity is determined by geography or by family status, the increased importance of formal education in modern America tends to make for social stratification" (Conant, 1948, p. 41). Limited access to education had limited social mobility and, in the postwar, was increasing social inequality. If one had no access to schools because one did not live where they were readily available and if one's access to schooling was limited by one's membership in a racial group or one of the lower social classes, then equality of educational opportunity did not exist.

In *Study for the Ford Foundation on Policy and Program* (1949) that was prepared to satisfy a request made by the foundation's trustees in 1947, it was concluded that social mobility depended on equality of educational opportunity and that minorities were being denied educational opportunities. The trustees were advised that:

> In practice, education should accord equal opportunity to all. This is not only a fundamental democratic principle; it is a prerequisite to the social mobility and fluidity which are basic to democracy. Without equal educational opportunity, equality of economic opportunity can not exist. . . .

> Prejudice and discrimination abridge the educational opportunities of the members of our minority groups. Persons of all races and colors do not have equal access to education. The advantages of education are also walled off behind economic barriers, which are even more prevalent though perhaps less well publicized. . . .[2]

In early 1945, as World War II was nearing its end, the United States Senate Committee on Education and Labor held hearings on a proposal to provide federal aid for public education. As had earlier proposals, the proposal then failed. However, the hearings constituted a sign that public education was acquiring a place on the national agenda and that what Diane Ravitch (1983) identified as the "major theme" of the hearings—"the lack of equal opportunity in American education" (p. 5)—would be high on the national agenda for the remainder of the twentieth century and beyond. The testimony presented to the Senate committee documented the disparities in support for the nation's public schools, especially the differences in how schools in the North were supported as opposed to those in the South and how the schools to which African Americans were assigned were not nearly as well supported as those to which whites were assigned.

Edwin R. Embree had already reported the differences between the African American schools and the white schools.[3] In 1935–1936, a survey of southern states revealed that the annual expenditure per pupil was "$17.04 for Negro children and $49.30 for white children" (Embree, 1942, p. 38). Embree's findings were repeated in Gunnar Myrdal's report for the Carnegie Corporation, *An American Dilemma* (1944). Myrdal's study also showed that economic, social, political, and educational opportunities were severely limited for African Americans. Given that Americans have seen schooling as a primary vehicle for social and economic mobility, the limitations for educational opportunities for African Americans were remarkable, clearly discriminatory, and certainly not equal.

When Myrdal investigated the support for education for whites and for African Americans, he found "that Negro [*sic*] schools have lately been improving faster than white schools in the South—that is, in the sense that the *percentage* of increase in expenditures may have been greater for Negro [*sic*] than for white schools" (Myrdal, 1962, p. 342). However, the improvements were not great enough to overcome the already vast differences that had been established in the previous half-century. The differences in the support for the schools for whites and the schools for African Americans were "as spectacular as it is well known." The differences in expenditures affected all areas of public education. African American teachers' salaries were lower than those of white teachers and their classes were larger. Less was spent on transportation of African American students than for whites. "Savings" were realized in African American schools in all areas by maintaining a school year that was "thirteen percent shorter than in white schools" (Myrdal, 1962, pp. 339–340).

If the measure or definition of equality opportunity is resources, it may be possible to argue that equality of educational opportunity did not exist in the 1940s and still does not exist. In a 2006 report of how American students performed on the Program for International Student Assessment (PISA), it was shown that there was a relationship between students' social-economic status and their scores. That report suggested that: "The exam's results are not surprising, given research showing that the U.S. system tends to provide underprivileged students with less demanding curricula, poorer-quality teachers, and fewer educational resources than their peers in wealthier U. S. Communities" (Cavanagh, 2007b, p. 13).

Underlying the documentation of the gross disparities in how schools for various populations and in various parts of the nation were supported that were reported by Embree, Myrdal, and the testimony before the Senate Committee were the beliefs that schools were important and that schools made a difference. Subsequently, the proposition that schools are capable of making a difference was challenged in *The Coleman Report* and then reaffirmed again in No Child Left Behind. In the 1940s, 1950s, and early 1960s it was generally believed that schools did make a difference. It was then believed that equal investments in schools would produce equal results and that students who attended equally supported schools would benefit equally. However, *The Coleman Report* "pointed indirectly to the inadequacy of previous educational evaluations that assumed a uniform cost/quality-relationship for public schools" (Ford Foundation, 1972, p. 12). To benefit equally would eventually mean that scores on standardized achievement tests would not show consistent differences between the scores of those classified as members of the dominant or majority group and those classified as belonging to one of the minority groups, or between disadvantaged students and those not so classified.

The *Brown* Decision. When the Supreme Court handed down the *Brown* decision in 1954, it was widely believed and widely reported that the Court had overturned *Plessy v. Ferguson* (1896) and that the dissent of Justice John Marshall Harlan who claimed that the United States Constitution was "color-blind" had been heard. That was not, however, the case. As Jack Greenberg (1994, p. 116) explained, "Nominally, the Court's only legal directive in *Brown* was that states might no longer segregate the races in schools."[4] The Court simply ruled that separate but equal in public education was unequal, violated the Fourteenth Amendment, and was therefore unconstitutional. Chief Justice Warren was aware of *Plessy*, discussed it, but did not overturn it and did not accept Justice Harlan's dissent in *Plessy*. Had he ruled on the basis of Harlan's dissent, he would have taken away the federal government's right to make and to acknowledge racial distinctions and to make color-conscious rulings. Warren did argue in *Bolling* that racial classifications "must be scrutinized with particular care, since they are contrary to our traditions and hence constitutionally suspect," but his position in *Brown* effectively held that racial classifications were not unconstitutional.

As Hugh Davis Graham (1990) observed, "Because *Brown* had stopped short of holding unconstitutional all racial classifications by government as impermissibly color-conscious per se, then, the Court was able to maximize its newly claimed authority and jurisdiction while minimizing limitations on its discretion in enforcing its decree and affording remedies" (p. 368). Had Chief Justice Warren sided with Justice Harlan's dissent in *Plessy*, the "performance criteria" (some called them quotas) that the Office of Education set down in March 1966 and were subsequently used by the federal courts to ensure that public schools would be desegregated would have been unconstitutional.

In the 1940s and 1950s many believed that legally sanctioned racial segregation of students in public schools denied African Americans access to the superior schools to which white students were assigned and thus denied them equality of educational opportunity. The *Brown* decision introduced another way to measure equality of educational opportunity that acquired significance in the mid-1960s, in the 1970s, and beyond. The new measure was integration. The Supreme Court ruled in favor of the plaintiffs in *Brown* not because the schools to which African-Americans were assigned were not as well supported as the schools to which white students were assigned. In fact, Robert Carter, the attorney who argued for the Kansas Plaintiffs, acknowledged that the facilities provided for African American children in Topeka were in fact equal to those provided for the white children. Rather than arguing that school districts failed to provide equal facilities for African Americans, Carter and the other Legal Defense Fund (LDF) attorneys, Thurgood Marshall, James Nabritt, and Jack Greenberg attacked the legality of segregation by attacking the doctrine of "separate but equal." They argued that the quality and thus equality of schooling depended on intangible considerations as well as tangible facilities. Quality and effectiveness depended on intangible considerations, such as the school's academic climate, the teaching standards, and the school's prestige.

To make their case, the LDF attorneys employed arguments developed by social and behavioral scientists. The defendants objected to the introduction of "sociological" evidence but the Court admitted the "extra-legal factors." Chief Justice Warren cited the "academic evidence"[5] in his decision. From that evidence, he concluded that to separate children on the basis of race creates "a feeling of inferiority" that probably could never be completely undone and thus has the effect of retarding the mental and educational progress of African American children. That, the Court unanimously decided, deprived those children of rights specified in the Fourteenth Amendment of the Constitution. Racial segregation in public schools constituted inequality and was therefore unconstitutional. The extent to which schools were racially integrated or segregated became a significant measure of equality of educational opportunity. That meant that students who were assigned to a racially segregated school even if the school was supported as well as all other schools were denied equality of educational opportunity. In the years immediately following *Brown*, given this new measure, there was not much equality of educational opportunity to measure, for there was little desegregation of the schools. Integration of the nation's public schools was successfully resisted because school district officials who wanted to avoid school desegregation took advantage of the "Briggs dictum" and because the Court's direction in *Brown II* on May 31, 1955 did not order immediate action.

Briggs Dictum and *Brown II*. In April 1955, in *Briggs v. Elliott* Judge John J. Parker of the Fourth Circuit Court of Appeals rendered an opinion—that came to be known as the "Briggs dictum—that maintained that the Constitution and the Supreme Court's ruling in *Brown* only prohibited deliberate segregation but did not require deliberate integration or deliberate desegregation of public schools. According to the "Briggs dictum," *Brown* did not interfere with the right of parents to choose the schools they wanted their children to attend. *Brown* did rule that school districts could no longer assign students to schools based on their race. However, school officials were able to implement pupil-placement plans whereby a student was allowed to request a transfer from one school to another according to the procedures specified in freedom-of-choice plans that many districts in the South soon designed and implemented. African American students' requests for transfer to another school were typically subject to presumably nonracial criteria. The criteria school systems adopted were applied in ways that resulted in few requests for transfer, and few requests for transfer were granted. School districts employed freedom-of-choice plans as a way to comply with *Brown* and, at the same time, to avoid any significant desegregation of public schools. Avoiding desegregation was denying equality of educational opportunity because the Supreme Court ruled that "separate but equal" was not equal.

Brown I (the May 17, 1954 decision), only ruled that racial segregation in public education was unconstitutional. Significantly, it provided no immediate relief for children who were required to attend racially segregated schools in neither the seventeen states that required segregation nor the four that permitted segregation.[6] The Court postponed deciding how and when its decision—a decision that appeared to require desegregation of public schools—would be implemented "because these are class actions, because of the wide applicability of this decision, because of the great variety of local conditions," and because "the formulation of decrees in these cases presents problems of considerable complexity." The court restored the case to the docket so decisions about implementation could be made and implemented.

Those who were unhappy with *Brown I* and wanted to resist desegregation found reason for hope in *Brown II* (May 31, 1955). While the Court ordered local school districts to "make a prompt and reasonable start toward full compliance" and to do so "at the earliest practicable date," it also recognized that school districts needed time to solve problems related to "administration, arising from physical condition of school plant, the school transportation system, personnel, revision of school districts and attendance areas into compact units to achieve a system of determining admission to the public schools on a nonracial basis, and revision of local laws and regulations which may be necessary in solving the foregoing problems." The Supreme Court assigned responsibility for overseeing the desegregation of schools to the federal district courts but provided neither clear guidelines nor deadlines. The federal district courts were to "enter such orders and decrees consistent with this opinion as are necessary and proper to admit to public schools on a racially nondiscriminatory basis *with all deliberate speed* the parties to these cases."

With all deliberate speed proved to mean neither soon nor immediately. By the end of the 1950s, the Legal Defense Fund had filed more than sixty cases to end racial segregation in elementary as well as high schools and most cases were still pending. As of June 1960, five southern states—Alabama, Georgia, Louisiana, Mississippi and South Carolina—managed not to admit any African American student to a school with white students (Greenberg, 1994, p. 255). As Hugh Davis Graham (1990) observed, "'with all deliberate speed' had led to a decade of southern intransigence marked by the barest tokenism" (p. 366). A decade after *Brown I*, the overwhelming majority of African American students were still attending racially segregated schools; only 2.3 percent of southern African American students were attending desegregated schools (p. 372). There was then little, if any, equality of educational opportunity, for "separate but equal" continued to be the rule rather than the exception.

A Cold War Decision. The Supreme Court's ruling in *Brown*, that separate but equal in public education was unequal and therefore unconstitutional, was a modest beginning toward resolving the problem— "the lack of equal opportunity in American education" that had been identified by Embree, in *Who Shall Be Educated?*, in Myrdal's *American Dilemma*, at the 1945 Senate hearings, and the 1949 Ford Foundation report. Those who testified that differences between the support provided for the schools to which white students were assigned and the support provided for the schools to which African Americans were assigned within and between the various states served to maintain inequalities were effectively maintaining that it was in the nation's interest to address the inequalities. In the postwar era, it was becoming increasingly clear to American leaders that it was in the interest of the nation to extend equality of educational opportunity to those who were denied that opportunity because of racial discrimination.

In 1948 Conant argued that it was the duty of "thoughtful" Americans to "work toward a greater degree of educational opportunity for those groups which are held back because of racial prejudice in various sections of the nation." That the nation's ideals were "contradicted every time we segregate Negroes [*sic*] or discriminated against those of Mexican, Japanese, or Jewish ancestry" was, he maintained, "obvious." In addition, he maintained that the nation would be "a great deal better off if careers were freely open to all the talented" (Conant, 1948, pp. 67–68).

In *Brown* the Supreme Court clearly maintained that the federal government had an interest in public education, for it was then necessary to "consider public education in the light of its full development and its present place in American life throughout the Nation." The Court further observed that: "Compulsory school laws and the great expenditures for education both demonstrate our recognition of the importance of education to our democratic society." Education was the "foundation of good citizenship" and "required for the performance of our most basic public responsibilities, even service in the armed forces." The Court was expressing what would soon be even more explicitly expressed: National defense required educated citizens. The Court further explained that citizens could not be "expected to succeed in life" if they were "denied the opportunity of an education."[7] In the Cold War Era, education was necessary not only for the welfare of individual citizens but also the welfare of the nation. *Brown* showed an interest in the nation's need for knowledgeable human capital. It was also sensitive to the postwar political climate. As Jack Greenberg (1994) later observed, "international and political developments [had] inspired hope" (p. 68). It was becoming increasingly difficult to deny African Americans the rights and freedoms for which they had fought, often with distinction, during World War II.

Brown was decided during Dwight D. Eisenhower's presidency, but the case was filed during Harry S. Truman's administration. Truman's Justice Department filed an *amicus curiae* brief in support of the plaintiffs just weeks before Dwight D. Eisenhower took office. Its brief reminded the Court that "it is in the context of the present world struggle between freedom and tyranny that the problem of racial discrimination must be viewed" (quoted in Borstelmann, 2001, p. 93). The Justice Department's brief on the side of the plaintiffs in *Brown* was not its first participation in a school segregation case. Truman's administration took an active interest not only in the *Brown* case but also in other civil rights cases that reached the Supreme Court. Truman's Justice Department had earlier participated in two school segregation cases—*McLaurin v. Oklahoma State Regents for Higher Education* and *Sweatt v. Painter*—that paved the way for *Brown*. The Justice Department then argued that these cases were important because "they test the vitality and strength of the democratic ideals to which the United States is dedicated." The Justice Department asked the Supreme Court to consider how its ruling would affect the nation's foreign policy. Foreign policy considerations required that the nation put an end to racial discrimination (Dudziak, 2000, pp. 94–95). The message was clear: racial equality was necessary for national security (p. 104). For the Justice Department that relied heavily on communications from the State Department to construct its briefs, there was no question that *Brown* and *Bolling v. Sharpe* had "national security implications" (p. 101)

Truman's Justice Department could not claim any concrete interests in several civil rights cases but it did nevertheless file *amicus curiae* briefs in civil rights cases, emphasizing to the Court "the international implications of race discrimination and at times focused on the negative impact on U. S. foreign relations that a prosegregation decision might have." A decision that ruled that racial segregation was unconstitutional promised to have great and significant "symbolic value" (Dudziak, 2000, p. 90), for the nation that was then engaged in the Cold War. It was becoming increasingly difficult and embarrassing for the United States to object to European colonialism while the United States itself denied African Americans their rights in ways not very different from how colonial powers treated the nonwhite people they had colonized.

The Supreme Court's claim that the nation had an interest in public education that extended beyond the interests of states and localities where major responsibility for public education resided was further confirmed by the United States Congress in 1954. Besides passing the Cooperative Research Act (Public Law 83-531) that authorized cooperative arrangements with universities, colleges, and state educational agencies for educational research, it also created the National Advisory Committee on Education (Public Law 83-532) the purpose of which was to identify needed studies of national interest in the field of education and to recommend appropriate action indicated by the identified studies. It also authorized funds for President Eisenhower's 1955 White House Conference on Education, the first such conference ever held.

The 1955 White House Conference on Education

When President Eisenhower delivered his State of the Union address to the second session of the eighty-third Congress in January 1954, he called for each state and each territory to conduct a conference on education that was to culminate in the first White House Conference on Education in 1955. Congress agreed and authorized $700,000 to support the costs of statewide meetings that brought educators and citizens together to discuss what their schools needed. When Eisenhower wrote to the governors of the states about the state conferences on September 12, 1954, he indicated that the state conferences would constitute "the most thorough, widespread, and concerted study the American people have ever made of their educational problems" (quoted in Sundquist, 1968, pp. 157–158). On December 2, 1954 President Eisenhower met with the committee he had appointed for the White House Conference. The Committee, chaired by Procter and Gamble's president Neil H. McElroy[8] who was later appointed as Secretary of Defense, accepted three major responsibilities: to assist states and territories who asked for help in organizing their own conferences; to organize and conduct the White House Conference; and to prepare a report for the President on the "significant and pressing problems" the nation's elementary and secondary schools faced.

While Professor Arthur E. Bestor was making his case against what he believed the condition of American education was and arguing for what he believed should occur in the nation's schools, participants in the first White House Conference on Education met from November 28 through December 1, 1955 and presented a view different from what Bestor was advocating. The Committee for the White House Conference recognized and accepted that the goals for public education had "grown with increased speed" and that its "overall mission has been enlarged." The Committee identified fifteen "goals" public schools were being asked to accept and accomplish:

1. A general education as good as or better than that offered in the past, with increased emphasis on the physical and social sciences.
2. Programs designed to develop patriotism and good citizenship.
3. Programs designed to foster moral, ethical, and spiritual values.
4. Vocational education tailored to the abilities of each pupil and to the needs of community and Nation.
5. Courses designed to teach domestic skills.
6. Training in leisure-time activities such as music, dancing, vocational reading, and hobbies.
7. A variety of health services for all children, including both physical and dental inspections, and instruction aimed at bettering health knowledge and habits.
8. Special treatment for children with speech or reading difficulties and other handicaps.
9. Physical education, ranging from systematic exercises, physical therapy, and intramural sports, to interscholastic athletic competition.
10. Instruction to meet the needs of the abler students.
11. Programs designed to acquaint with countries other than their own in an effort to help them understand the problems America faces in international relations.
12. Programs designed to foster mental health.
13. Programs designed to foster wholesome family life.
14. Organized recreational and social activities.
15. Courses designed to promote safety. These include instruction in driving automobiles, swimming, civil defense, etc.

The Committee acknowledged that some viewed the new and expanded school goals with "dismay" but accepted them as "legitimate" (The Committee, 1956, pp. 8–9).

The "school goals" accepted by the Committee for the 1955 White House Conference constituted an acceptance of the seven cardinal principles presented by the Committee on the Reorganization of Secondary Education in 1918. The White House Committee agreed that the public schools had responsibilities that went beyond preparing students for college. However, it also called for an "increased emphasis" on the physical sciences and "instruction to meet the needs of the abler students," those whom *Life* identified as the "gifted" and those whom Conant identified as the "talented."

The Committee appointed by President Eisenhower included two "non-educators" for every educator, and the Committee urged the governors of the states and territories to adopt a similar ratio. The Committee's Report did not completely avoid recognition of either the need for equality of educational opportunity or the need for knowledgeable human capital. However, its structure and composition may explain why it so clearly reflected questions citizens and educators at the local and the state levels were trying to answer in the postwar years: What should the schools accomplish? How can schools be organized to be more efficient and economical? What are the needs for school buildings? How can qualified teachers be found and retained? How can the financing for building and operating schools be secured? How can the public's interest in education be obtained and maintained? The emphasis on the need for funding for new schools and for more teachers was understandable given that during the Great Depression and World War II, school districts were not able to invest in school plans and had lost teachers to either the armed forces or the war industries. After the War school officials knew they had to find additional classrooms to accommodate the baby boomers and more teachers to teach the baby boomers.

What was expressed in *Brown* was clearly stated at the White House Conference on Education. The Committee for the White House Conference reported that "one fundamental fact" had emerged: the schools' importance for the "welfare" of the nation had become "more important than ever before." Moreover, that importance had been "dangerously underestimated for a long time." The Committee saw a connection among educational opportunity, economic opportunity, and social mobility. There was recognition at the White House Conference that: "Nowadays equality of opportunity for adults means little without equality of educational opportunity for children" (The Committee, 1956, p. 9). Once the frontier closed, schools prevented "rigid class barriers" from developing. The availability of schools ensured that "a man is not frozen at any level of our economy, nor is his son" (p. 4).

The Committee also recognized what the nation needed to prosecute the Cold War, what it described as "this era of international stress." In his opening address, McElroy reminded the participants that education was clearly related to the nation's national defense:

> Think of the time in which we live! Within our own memory, we have been through two world wars and the Korean War. We are part of an age which obliges self-governing peoples to constantly arm themselves against the pos-

> sibility of a war of total destruction, or the even worse possibility of losing their freedom. In this highly technical era, education has become as much a part of our system of defense as the Army, the Navy, or the Air force. We must have good schools, not only because of our ideals, but for survival. (National Association of School Principals, 1956, pp. 141–142)

In his address to the White House Conference participants, Vice-President Richard M. Nixon drew their attention to the claims of Admiral Lewis Strauss, Chairman of the United States Atomic Energy Commission, who maintained the nation was confronting a crisis in the training of scientists and engineers. Admiral Strauss indicated that if the present trend continued to 1960, the Soviet Union would have trained 300,000 more new scientists and engineers than the United States. Strauss expressed concern that over half the nation's high schools offered courses in neither chemistry nor physics, that less than 5 percent of high school students enrolled in physics compared to 20 percent in 1890, that only 25 percent enrolled in algebra compared to 50 percent in 1890, that there was a 30 percent decrease in students who were studying chemistry, and between 250,000 and 400,000 students were receiving instruction in mathematics from teachers not trained in the subject.

Nixon also agreed with Admiral Hyman Rickover who asserted: "If the crisis in education is not met, we will be in danger of losing the cold war." For Nixon there was no question that "our national security has a tremendous stake in our educational system" (National Association, 1956, p. 148). In addition to the "unusual demands for good scientists and engineers . . . and other specialists," there was a demand for citizens who knew the "meaning of citizenship" and "who know something of other nations and are equipped to understand their own Nation's role in international affairs" (The Committee, 1956, p. 12).

The Committee for the White House Conference acknowledged the Supreme Court's *Brown* decision. For the Committee that decision related to one of "two problems" over which there were disagreements that were not then easily resolved "partly because of the limited time at its disposal for complete discussion of the many intricacies of the different points of view represented on the committee." Those two problems were "religion" and "segregation." For the Committee the Supreme Court seemed not to offer clear and concise directions on either problem. Court rulings on "church-state relations" appeared to clarify "only small parts of the whole question." According to the Committee, "the relationship of the issue of segregation to the generally accepted goal of equal educational opportunity" was "an area of conflicting opinions not entirely resolved by Supreme Court action"

(The Committee, 1956, p. 10). The Committee's position was consistent with what the Supreme Court declared in *Brown II*. The Committee agreed: "that the great social, psychological, and organizational changes implicit in the recent decisions of the Supreme Court designed to abolish [racial] segregation in the public schools cannot be achieved with equal speed in every community." It was a problem that had to "be worked out by each community in its own way within the framework of existing legal structures and the intent of the relevant Supreme Court decisions" (p. 10).

In his remarks at the close of the conference McElroy indicated that "fair play for everyone" was a "driving force" and acknowledged that equality of educational opportunity was an "emotional" as well as an important issue:

> We all recognize that the schools have become this nation's most powerful instrument for preserving equality of opportunity—opportunity of all kinds. The schools are perhaps the chief expression of this country's desire to treat everyone fairly. We Americans believe in competition, but in fair, unhandicapped [*sic*] competition only. The material rewards our economy offers are closely geared to an individual's ability and capacity for hard work. Let people do as well as they can, we say, but let them all begin as evenly as possible. There is a patent unfairness about allowing some people to have their talents and attitudes cultivated during childhood, and allowing others to be neglected. That unfairness is abhorrent to all of us. We feel a fundamental lack of justice in poor schools, and that is why so many of us rally to improve education. That is one major reason why educational problems are so emotional.... (National Association, 1956, p. 150)

McElroy also reminded the participants that the nation's "schools are necessary for survival," and that "industry," "agriculture," and the "armed forces" all depended on "educated men" (National Association, 1956, p. 150). The nation's schools were expected to produce the knowledgeable human capital that the nation's defense and economy required.

President's Committee on Education Beyond High School

The White House Conference on Education only considered the needs of elementary and secondary education. It had no charge to consider the needs and problems of higher education. President Eisenhower responded to those concerned with higher education in the spring of 1956 by appointing the President's Committee on Education Beyond the High School. The former president of the Carnegie Corporation, Devereux C. Josephs who was then Chairman of the Board of the New York Life Insurance Company, served as chairman of the thirty-five member committee, and University of Illinois president David D. Henry served as vice chairman.[9] In November 1966 the Committee submitted a first "tentative" report in which it observed that the increased birth rate of the previous fifteen years that was placing "enormous strains on elementary and secondary schools" would soon place a similar strain on higher education, and a "great expansion" of the capacity of higher education was necessary. It also reported on the need for knowledgeable human capital or as the committee expressed it, "there are rapidly increasing demands throughout our expanding economy for men and women with education and training beyond the high school" (The President's Committee, 1957, p. ix).

The committee held five regional meetings in the fall of 1956 at which 200 hundred citizens and educators helped to set an agenda for five regional conferences. Several agencies or associations[10] agreed to cosponsor one of the five regional conferences held in April and May 1957. Nearly 1,400 invited participants who represented "a cross section of outstanding lay and professional leadership from all the States and Territories" attended the regional conferences (The President's Committee, 1957, p. x).

On July 27, 1957, ten weeks before the Soviet Union launched *Sputnik*, the committee transmitted its final, or second report, to the president. As were others, the committee was aware that the nation had entered, indeed had been "propelled," into a "new educational era" after World War II. The new educational era that presented challenges that the nation was not yet prepared to meet was brought about by a knowledge explosion, a population explosion, technological and economic advances, "the outbreak of ideological conflict and the uprooting of old political and cultural patterns on a worldwide scale," and Americans' demands for more education and better education. In addition, the nation had no choice but to face the challenges the Soviet Union presented:

> America would be heedless if she closed her eyes to the dramatic strides being taken by the Soviet Union in post-high school education, particularly in the development of scientists, engineers and technicians. She would be inexcusably blind if she failed to see that the challenge of the next 20 years will require leaders not only in science and engineering and in business and industry, but in government and politics, in foreign affairs and diplomacy, in education and civic affairs. A responsible exercise of our Nation's role in world leadership also requires a broadened citizen interest in and understanding of foreign relations and world affairs. (The President's Committee, 1957, p. 1)

The "gap" between what the nation was providing and what it needed to provide required attention, for it was "widening ominously."

The Committee made a direct connection among its conclusion that colleges and universities needed more teachers, the need to end discrimination against women and minorities, and the need to expand educational opportunities. Women constituted a great pool of future college and university teachers, and higher education needed to "overcome the cultural attitudes which have consigned women to a decided minority role in the ranks of higher education." Not to recognize the contributions women were able to make was "an enormous waste of brain power" that was not unlike the waste that resulted "wherever employment barriers exist against members of racial and religious minorities" (The President's Committee, 1957, p. 7). Women who were as well qualified as men to continue their education beyond high school were less likely to do so. One study of 10, 830 "fully qualified" students showed that 42 percent of qualified boys did not go on to full-time study after high school graduation and that 58 percent of the girls did not do so (p. 44).

Like President Truman's Commission on Higher Education, the Committee estimated "at least 50 percent of all high school graduates could benefit from some type of formal education beyond high school" (The President's Committee, 1957, p. 9). That estimate required expanding educational opportunity, and for the Committee, expanding educational opportunity meant not only attending to what was necessary so that the 200,000 "of the ablest young people" who each year did not attend school beyond high school would do so but also removing "discriminatory barriers." That the doors of educational opportunity to many able students were closed "because of race, creed, origin or sex" was "intolerable under democratic principles." The committee further recommended that "educational institutions abolish discriminatory polices and practices based on race, creed, color, sex or national origin, where they exist" (pp. 8, 18).

Minority group students had fewer opportunities to continue their education after high school, and those who managed to complete their post-high school education had fewer opportunities after doing so. According to the committee:

> Educational opportunities throughout the Nation are not always fully accessible to minority group members. Not only are there cases of overt discrimination in admission and after admission in access to curricular or extracurricular opportunities, but—perhaps more widely important—there are discriminatory employment practices which discourage some of these young people from seeking advanced education. (The President's Committee, 1957, p. 44)

The nation's discriminatory practices were effectively reducing its supply of knowledgeable human capital.

It was clear to the Committee that the nation was not adequately developing all its talent. Economic inequalities and discriminatory practices were producing significant inequality of educational opportunity. The Committee reported that: "The percentages of able high school graduates not continuing their education beyond high school are especially high among children of nonprofessional parents, minority groups, girls, and rural and low-income families." The Committee cited a study that revealed that the social class of one's parents was a good predictor of which students were likely to attend college. While "92 percent of the high-ability sons of professional workers planned to attend college," only 69 percent of the high-ability sons of factory workers had similar plans. While "81 percent of all sons of professional workers planned to attend college," only 30 percent of all sons of factory workers, had similar plans. Another study clearly showed that "a youth who is academically in the lower half of his graduating class, and whose family income is $9,000 or more, is more likely to go to college than a youth in the upper fourth of his class and in a family with income of less than $5,000" (The President's Committee, 1957, pp. 43, 45).

The Rockefeller Panel Report

In 1956, the Rockefeller Brothers Fund, having observed that the United States had made extraordinary progress in its "domestic development" and "had emerged as the strongest nation and the best hope of freedom in an explosive world," concluded that it was necessary for the nation to "shape events through its own sense of purpose." So that the nation would not "be engulfed in events shaped by others, " the Fund organized The Special Studies Project. Between January 1958 and September 1960 the Project issued six reports, the fifth of which, issued on June 26, 1958 addressed education. Report V, "The Pursuit of Excellence: Education and the Future of America," "written principally" by the chair of the panel, John W, Gardner,11 president of the Carnegie Corporation of New York emphasized that the nation needed to recognize that education was more important than ever before, was not as good as it needed to be, and that its importance had to be recognized:

> We have always told one another, sometimes with an all too shallow piety, that education is a vital element in the strength of our society. The times have grimly underscored the correctness of that view. But it is no longer sufficient to repeat it as an incantation. We must recognize that in many areas our

educational facilities are poor and our educational effort slovenly. (Report V, 1961, p. 361)

Like other such reports in the Cold War Era, Panel V's Report focused on the nation's need for knowledgeable human capital, the need to identify and cultivate gifted students, the importance of equality of opportunity, and the nation's failure to extend opportunities to women and minorities. It also addressed the condition and the role of education and the presumed tension between equality and quality.

Knowledgeable Human Capital. Panel V observed that the "explosive rate of technological change and the increasing complexity of our social organization" had resulted in "a great variety of shortages of human resources in fields requiring high competence and extended training." The nation had to recognize "the long-term trend toward greater demand for trained manpower," and the need to attend to the quantity and the quality of the talent it needed. It was necessary to view the nation's "human resources" "as a vast reservoir of human abilities and skills upon which our social and technical and economic institutions depend[ed]" (Report V, 1961, pp. 345–346), and it was education that provided individuals with the abilities and skills they required. "The ablest students are often exposed to educational programs whose content is too thin and whose pace is too slow to challenge their abilities," because many educators objected to tracking or grouping students based on their ability (p. 363). It was necessary to abandon "the notion that either a flexible promotion policy or a flexible curricular arrangements are undemocratic in spirit" (p. 372).

The skill and the training the labor force would require in the future were "expected to accelerate." Professional soldiers could no longer be totally responsible for "military strategy," for it was then also relying on "advice of scholars and technical experts." Government was increasingly relying on "the talents of the economist, the agronomist, the public health officer, and similar experts." The nation's economy had been successful because of its "willingness to innovate," and innovation depended on research that depended on the nation's talent. "The Soviet military threat" also made systematic research an imperative for the nation. "Technological inferiority" was a danger that threatened the nation's survival. The nation's "cultivation of human resources" was necessary "to maintain the strength and vitality and growth potential of our society" (Report V, 1961, pp. 348–349, 351).

The Gifted. The Panel reported that the nation had come to the realization that it had paid "too little attention to the individual of unusual talent or potentialities." The nation had to seek to identify talent and to ensure that it was properly cultivated. To suggest that the nation had not done enough to identify and to cultivate talent was "not to deplore the unprecedented time and money we have devoted to raising the general level of achievement" (Report V, 1961, p. 355). The gifted were not to be served at the expense of all others. To identify and cultivate the talent the nation required, it was necessary to end the discrimination women and African Americans suffered, to attend to testing programs and guidance programs capable of identifying talent, the quality of the education the nation provided, the curriculum the schools offered talented individuals, and what was required of talented students.

The Panel clearly wanted to "demand the best of our most gifted, most talented, and most spirited youngsters." It estimated that 15 to 20 percent of high school students were "capable of high caliber college work." It predicted that from the "top 2 percent" "will come many of the young men and women who will reach the pinnacles of intellectual achievement and creativity in the years ahead." For "high caliber" students the Panel endorsed the College Entrance Examination Board's Advanced Placement Program and "the experimental Program for Early Admission to College, under which about 1,000 able students have entered twelve different colleges over the last five years *before* completing the last year or two of high school" (Report V, 1961, pp. 372–373).

Inadequate Use of Talent: Women and African Americans. Panel V's Report (1961) appeared only two years after the *Brown* decision and one year after *Brown II*, and the Panel clearly acknowledged the significance of *Brown*. For the Panel, "the end of segregation, with all the difficult adjustments it imposes, is of course a step in the right direction. The economic, political, and social disadvantages visited upon African Americans had "until recently been thought of solely in terms of an abrogation of moral principle." However, in light of the nation's requirements for knowledgeable human capital, denying African Americans their right to equality of educational opportunity resulted "in the loss of potentially creative and skillful manpower" (p. 381).

Panel V reported that the National Manpower Council reported that a third of the nation's labor force were women and their role was becoming "increasingly important." However, women were underutilized in the labor force. While it was the case that women were "typically less well prepared for careers than men," it was also the case that women were "faced with other handicaps of a less formal but more prejudicial nature." Some firms were hesitant to employ women in "executive capacities" and they were excluded from "executive training programs." For a variety of reasons, women were not as well prepared to participate in the labor force, and "no improvement is likely to occur until there are substantially better opportunities for the gifted women to find an occupation suitable to her capacities" (Report V, 1961, p. 382).

The Panel reported that President Eisenhower had asked Congress to support the nation's depressed areas and that he did so "on grounds of equity." According to the Panel, it was clear that children who grew up in depressed areas turned out not to be as well prepared to serve the nation as those who grew up in other areas. Fore example, "During the first year of the Korean conflict, the national failure rate on the Armed Forces Qualification Test was 19.2 per cent, but the failure rate for men from nine states were incomes and educational expenditures are relatively low ranged from 34 to 58 per cent." Poor education was producing "a wastage of human abilities" that the Panel believed "should be of serious concern to the whole nation (Report V, 1961, pp. 382–383).

Testing and Guidance. To identify talent, it was appropriate to employ "large-scale testing programs." Testing programs were appropriate for large numbers of students to uncover talent that might "otherwise go unnoticed." Even when large numbers of students were not involved, testing was appropriate, for tests were capable of identifying an individual's talent or aptitude that would "escape the attention of all but the keenest of teachers" (Report V, 1961, p. 369). Tests were "most effective in measuring academic aptitude and achievement." Tests were to be part of "a strong guidance program" designed to identify a student's "educational programs" and "the most appropriate course of study for him." Guidance was to be used "to stimulate the individual to make the most of his potentialities" (p. 370). Schools needed "guidance officers" to assist teachers.

Equality of Opportunity. The Panel believed in equality and emphasized that equality of opportunity was essentially a moral value. However, belief in equality did not mean a belief that all were "equal in all respects." Individual differences had to be recognized and accepted, for "men are unequal in their native capacities and their motivations, and therefore in their attainments" (Report V, 1961, pp. 355–356). According to the Panel:

> If we are really serious about equality of opportunity, we shall be serious about individual differences because what constitutes opportunity for one man is a stone wall for the next. If we are to do justice to the individual, we must seek for him the level and kind of education that will open *his* eyes, stimulate *his* mind, and unlock *his* potentialities. We should seek to develop many educational patterns—each geared to the particular capacities of the student for whom it is designed. (Report V, 1961, p. 373)

While recognizing that there were differences among people, the nation's conception of and its commitment to equality of opportunity required that all had equal access to education so they could use their talents to excel and to achieve. Differences in talent were "not judgments of differences in human worth" (Report V, 1961, p. 365). The nation had and was continuing to use its "educational system as the basic instrument for realizing our ideal of equality of opportunity" (p. 359).

The Panel recognized that individuals' social circumstances often severely limited their ability to achieve and to excel. "Each year many thousands of young people with the ability to do well in college fail to go beyond high school." Why so many failed to attend college was explained not only by their inability to finance their education. In addition, and perhaps equally important, "for a good many the primary reason is that their family and neighborhood environment have not provided them with the motivation and values that produce educational ambition" (Report V, 1961, p. 359).

Equality and Quality. Panel V rejected any claim that a choice among equality, quantity, and quality had to be made. The nature of American society was such that it had to commit the schools to "the maximum development of individual potentialities *at all levels*" (Report V, 1961, p. 362). The Panel saw no "incompatibility" in the demand for "excellence" and the demand "to educate everyone up to the level of his ability." The nation needed "an ample supply of high caliber scientists, mathematics, and engineers," and it needed "quantity" and "quality" (p. 368). "By insisting that *equality* means an exactly similar exposure to education, regardless of the variations in interest and capacity of the student, we are, in fact, inflicting a subtle but serious form of inequality upon our young people" (p. 363). "The Panel emphasized that "the schools cannot do full justice to each young person in developing what gifts he may possess until they face frankly the need to provide different programs for different types and levels of ability." The nation's schools had "made far more progress in *identifying* different levels of talent than in the *development of programs* for these different levels" (p. 371).

The Condition and Role of Education. Because it was necessary to seek and to cultivate talent, education had become strategically important to the nation. The Panel reported that in 1955 there were eighty times as many high school students than there were in 1870 while the nation's population had only increased fourfold. The increased high-school enrollment presented educators with new and expanded responsibilities. They had "to include in the curriculum an incredible variety of subjects, to take over more and more of the functions of the home, and to a accept a sense of responsibility for every psychic or civic crisis involving individuals below the age of consent." By the 1950s, it was clear that educators were faced not only with the responsibility of serving an increasing number of students but also with the responsibility to "offer higher quality in education." "Our schools are overcrowded, understaffed, and ill-equipped. In the fall of 1957, the shortage of public school classrooms stood at 142,000. There were 1,943,000 pupils in excess of "normal" classroom capacity." Besides more money, schools needed "an unsparing reexamination of current practices, patterns of organization, and objectives" (Report V, 1961, p. 361). The quality of the corps of teaches needed improvement. In 1956, 33 percent of elementary school teachers did not have a bachelor's degree and more than 21 percent of all teachers did not have a bachelor's degree. More graduate education was needed for teachers. Teachers needed to be relieved of "petty tasks," technology needed to be employed, and teachers need to be paid adequately.

The Curriculum. Panel V's recommendations for the school curriculum were "partly based" on "a recent study by Dr. James B. Conant" and on "the findings of a conference sponsored by the National Education Association on 'Education of the Academically Talented'" (Report V, 1961, p. 367). The Panel wanted all high school students to have "four years of English, three to four years of social studies, one year of mathematics, and one year of science. For the "academically talented student," the Panel recommended "two to three additional years of science, three additional years of mathematics, and at least three years of a foreign language." For some students, it was recommended that they study a second foreign language for three years in place of the fourth year of mathematics and a third year of science. The further panel observed that the mathematics curriculum and the science curriculum were being reformed and suggested other subjects needed to be modernized and have their quality improved. They wanted the "best minds" in the various fields to attend to those revisions and reforms.

Science Education. The Panel agreed that there was a "crisis" in science education but disagreed that the crisis was an "invention" of "the newspapers, or scientists, or the Pentagon." It also rejected the claim that the Soviet Union was the "cause" of the crisis in science education but did admit that the Soviet Union did, however, serve "as a rude stimulus to awaken" the nation into the new reality (Report V, 1961, p. 368). "The cause was the nation's "breathtaking movement into a new technological era."

The Need for Excellence. While the Panel clearly called for improved educational opportunities, it also wanted the nation to commit itself to excellence. It was not satisfied with the prevailing "images of citizen-as-consumer and citizen-as-constituent" (Report V, 1961, p. 390). It wanted all of society's educational institutions—home, church, school, and government—"to enable young people to see themselves as participants in one of the most exciting eras in history and to have a sense of purpose in relation to it." The Panel wanted youth to see that they faced not only a grave crisis but also "a time of great opportunity" (pp. 388–389).

Notes

1. See for example: *Pearson v. Murray (1936); Missouri ex rel. Gaines v. Canada (1938); Sipuel v. Oklahoma State Regents (1948); Sweatt v. Painter (1950)* and *McLaurin v. Oklahoma State Regents (1950).* For a brief discussion of these and their relationship to the Margold Report and the *Brown* decision see Richardson and Johanningmeier (2003, pp. 198–2003).
2. Quoted in *a foundation goes to school: The Ford Foundation Comprehensive School Improvement Program 1960–1970* (1972, p. 7).
3. Edwin R. Embree served as president of the Rosenwald Fund, 1917–1936.
4. However, soon afterwards the Supreme Court struck down state laws that required racial segregation on beaches, busses, parks, and golf courses, citing *Brown* by *per curiam* decisions that cited *Brown.*
5. The "academic evidence" the Court accepted included reports of research conducted by psychologists Kenneth Clark and Mamie Clark.
6. Racially segregated education was required in Alabama, Arkansas, Delaware, Florida, Georgia, Kentucky, Louisiana, Maryland, Mississippi, Missouri, North Carolina, Oklahoma, South Carolina, Tennessee, Texas, Virginia, West Virginia, and the District of Columbia. Arizona, Kansas, New Mexico, and Wyoming had laws that permitted racially segregated schools.
7. *Brown et al. v. Board of Education of Topeka et al.* 347I/S (1954) reproduced in Cohen (1974, p. 3105).
8. The other members of the committee were: Finnis E. Engleman, Connecticut State Commissioner of Education who served as vice-chairman; Mildred C. Ahlgren, past president, General Federation of Women's Clubs; Ethel G. Brown, president, National Congress of Parents and Teachers; Ralph J. Bunche, Under Secretary, United Nations; John S. Burke, president, B. Altman & Co.; John Cowles, president, *Minneapolis Star & Tribune*; John A. Hannah, president, Michigan State University; James W. Hargrove, vice president, Texas Eastern Transmission Corp.; Albert J. Hayes, president, International Association of Machinists; Margaret Hickey, editor, Public Affairs Department, *Ladies Home Journal*; Henry H. Hill, president, George Peabody College for Teachers; Oveta Culp Hobby, president, *The Houston Post*; Mildred McA. Horton, past president, Wellesley College; James R. Killian, Jr., president, Massachusetts Institute of Technology; Allan B. Kline, past president, American Farm Bureau; W. Preston Lane, Jr., ex-governor of Maryland; Roy E. Larsen, president and director, Time, Inc., past chairman, National Citizens Commission for the Public Schools; Thomas Lazzio, president, Local 300, UAW-CIO; Joseph C. McLain, principal Mamaroneck Senior High School; William E. McManus, assistant director, Department of Education, National

Catholic Welfare Conference; Lorimer D. Milton, president, Citizen Trust Co., Don G. Mitchell, chairman of board, Sylvania Electric Products, Inc.; Frank C. Moore, president, Government Affairs Foundation, Inc.; Herschel D. Newsome, master, National Grange; William S. Paley, chairman of board, Columbia Broadcasting System, Inc.; James F. Redmond, New Orleans superintendent of schools; Martha Shull, teacher and first vice president, National Education Association; Frank H. Sparks, president, Wabash College; Potter Stewart, judge, U. S. Court of Appeals; Jesse G. Stratton, past president, National School Boards Association, Inc., chairman of board, Minneapolis-Honeywell Regulator Co.; H. Grant Vest, Colorado State Commissioner of Educator; and Mayme E. Williams, teacher and president, National Congress of Colored Parents and Teachers. President Eisenhower served as Honorary Chairman. Marion B. Folsom, Secretary of Health, Education, and Welfare and S. M. Brownell, U. S. Commissioner of Education served as Honorary Vice Chairmen.

9. Other members of the committee were: Albert F. Arnason, Commissioner, North Dakota Board of Higher Education; George P. Berry, Dean, Harvard Medical School; Lawrence L. Bethel, President, Fashion Institute of Technology; Horace M. Bond, President, Lincoln University; Sydney P. Brown, Attorney, Member, Chicago Board of Education; Samuel Miller Brownell, Superintendent, Detroit Public Schools; Harold C. Case, President, Boston University; Dorothy Buffum Chandler, Assistant to the President, Times-Mirror Co., Los Angeles; Catherine B. Cleary, Vice President, First Wisconsin Trust; John D. Connors, Director, AFL-CIO Department of Education; Arthur G. Coons, President, Occidental College; J. Broward Culpepper, Executive Director, Board of Control of Florida Institutions of Higher Learning; Arthur Hollis Edens, President, Duke University; Paul L. Essert, Professor of Education, Columbia University; Crawford H. Greenwalt, President, E. I. du Pont de Nemours & Co., Inc.; Leo A, Hoegh, Former Governor of Iowa; Frederick L. Houde, President, Purdue University; Robert R. Hudelson, Former Dean, College of Agriculture, University of Illinois; Rees H. Hughes, President, Kansas State Teachers College; Seymour H. Knox, Chairman of Board, Marine Trust Company of Western New York; Roy E. Larsen, President, Time, Inc.; Katherine E. McBride, President, Bryn Mawr College; James McKinney, Chairman of Board, American School; James Lewis Morrill, President, University of Minnesota; Kenneth E. Oberholtzer, Superintendent, Denver Public Schools; Howard C. Petersen, President, Fidelity-Philadelphia Trust Co.; Paul C. Reinert, S. J., President, Saint Louis University; Dean M. Schweickhard, Commissioner of Education, State of Minnesota; Edgar W. Smith, Chairman, Governor's Committee on Higher Education in Oregon; Edgar B. Stern, Trustee, Tulane University; Anna Lord Strauss, Past National President, League of Women Voters; Laurence F. Whittemore, Chairman of Board, Brown Co.; and Theodore O. Yntema, Vice President, Ford Motor Co.

10. They included: The Western Interstate Commission for Higher Education, the Southern Regional Education Board, the North Central Association of Colleges and Secondary Schools, the Middle States Association of Colleges

and Secondary Schools, the New England Association of Colleges and Secondary Schools, and the New England Board of Higher Education.

11. Other Panel V members were: J. Douglas Brown, dean of faculty, Princeton University and former member, Mobilization Program Advisory Committee, Office of Defense Mobilization; Lowell T. Coggeshall, dean of the Division of Biological Sciences, University of Chicago and former special assistant for health and medical affairs, Department of Health, Education, and Welfare; Philip H. Coombs, secretary and director of research, The Fund for the Advancement of Education, Ford Foundation and former executive director, President's Materials Policy Commission; Dana L. Farnsworth, director, university health services, Harvard University and Radcliffe College and president, Group for the Advancement of Psychiatry; Eli Ginzberg, professor of economics, Columbia University and director of staff studies, National Manpower Council; Caryl P. Haskins, president, Carnegie Institution of Washington; Theodore M. Hesburg, president University of Notre Dame and commissioner, Civil Rights Commission; Margaret Hickey, public affairs editor, *Ladies' Home Journal*; David Riesman, professor, sociology department, University of Chicago; J. E. Wallace Sterling, president, Stanford University; Howard E. Wilson, dean School of Education, University of California, Los Angeles; Dael Wolfle, executive officer, American Association for the Advancement of Science and editor of *America's Resources of Specialized Talent*; Fred M. Hechinger, associate publisher, *Bridgeport Herald* and education editor, *Parents' Magazine*; and James R. Killian, Jr., president Massachusetts Institute of Technology.

5

Education for the Nation's Defense

Introduction

After the Soviet Union's successful launch of *Sputnik*, President Eisenhower asked the Congress to provide funds to improve public education in those areas essential for the national defense. Congress quickly overcame its traditional reluctance, if not outright refusal to provide support for public education, and passed the National Defense Education Act. Funds were soon available to improve and update the curricula and the instruction in those subjects believed to be directly related to the nation's defense capability: mathematics, science, and foreign language. So that the nation would have the intelligence required for successful competition with the Soviets in the Cold War, funds were provided to improve and upgrade the social science subjects. So that the talented or gifted students could be identified and efficiently and appropriately prepared to bolster the nation's defense capabilities, funds were made available to improve and expand the public schools' capabilities in guidance and testing. After *Sputnik*, those who had wanted the schools organized to produce knowledgeable human capital were seeing their agenda realized.

Equality of Educational Opportunity and Knowledgeable Human Capital, pages 73–106

By the mid-1960s, the interest in reforming the nation's schools, especially its high schools, and interest in identifying and serving those students identified as talented or gifted waned considerably as attention was directed toward waging war on poverty and providing improved educational opportunities for those students labeled as disadvantaged or underprivileged. There was a widespread belief or argument, tacit if not explicit, that public education could be organized to identify and serve the talented or the gifted students or it could direct its attention and resources to equity or equality, to improving services and opportunities for the disadvantaged or under privileged but it could not do both. Significantly, the proposition that the public education was confronted with an either-or proposition, that it had to choose between quality and equality, was forcefully and effectively challenged by Melvin M. Tumin and Marvin Bressler in their assessment of the proceedings of a conference hosted by Princeton University's Council on Human Relations in 1966. They held that the participants in the "Great Debate" of the previous decade failed to address adequately the issues of quality and equality. They denied that the desire to win the space race justified not providing all children with an equal quality education. They also questioned the efficacy and the propriety of many common school practices—for example, stereotyping, tracking, grading, and testing—that appeared to advantage some students and to penalize others.

Sputnik

On October 4, 1957, the Soviet Union placed a satellite in an earth orbit. It was named *Sputnik* that means "fellow traveler" in Russian. About once every hour and a half, the 184-pound sphere with a diameter of nearly twenty-three inches circled the earth and sent back signals every .3 seconds.1 *Sputnik* indicated to critics of American education and others concerned with the nation's defense and scientific capabilities that the Soviets had made significant advances in rocketry. On November 3, 1957, the Soviets dealt American prestige a second and a harsher blow when it launched *Sputnik II*. The Soviet's second satellite circled earth in a higher orbit than the first satellite and weighted six times more than the first *Sputnik*. It also contained an air-conditioned apartment carrying a live dog.

Sputnik, like Little Rock, was a "blow" to the nation's prestige throughout the world. Reports from American officials abroad reported that *Sputnik* did overshadow events in Little Rock (Dudziak, 2000, p. 145). In the United States, *Sputnik* drew some attention away from the five hundred paratroopers of the 101st Airborne Division President Eisenhower sent on September 24 to Little Rock to enforce a federal court order and to escort the nine

African American students into Central High. However, the Soviets were able to connect the situation in Little Rock and *Sputnik* by announcing to the world when *Sputnik* would pass over Little Rock.

Sputnik gave educators a new mission: "excellence" in education. Education discourse soon focused on how to implement the recommendations for the comprehensive high school proposed by James B. Conant in the *American High School Today* (1959a) and how to revise curricula to emphasize the structure of knowledge Jerome S. Bruner claimed was so essential in *The Process of Education* (1961). The claims of those who had earlier endorsed the Prosser Resolution—that the traditional high school was inappropriate for over half the nation's youth—were forgotten.

Those who had been criticizing the nation's public schools for not placing sufficient emphasis on standards and the traditional academic disciplines, especially mathematics, science, and foreign languages, were given instantaneous credibility by *Sputnik.* They were no longer seen as antidemocratic enemies of public education. Schools were now expected to produce the scientists and engineers the 1955 White House Conference participants, the President's Committee on Education Beyond the High School, and others had identified as needed. Public schools were to produce the knowledgeable human capital needed to win the arms race and the race to the moon.

Soviet success in rocketry was attributed to its allegedly superior educational system.[2] The apparent second place status of the United States in the space race was attributed to the nation's public schools that had strayed too far from the academic disciplines. *Sputnik* convinced many leaders that the time had come to reform the nation's public schools so the nation could take the lead in the space race. National defense, national security, and national prestige required nothing less. However, it should be noted that the educational reforms and the concerns with the nation's supply of knowledgeable human capital that are often attributed to *Sputnik* originated years before *Sputnik.* As early as 1950, "major industrial and professional groups" were already beginning "to feel the manpower pinch, particularly with respect to highly educated persons." Dwight D. Eisenhower, as president of Columbia University, had already "launched a major manpower study under the direction of Eli Ginzberg." In addition, the Central Intelligence Agency (CIA) and the National Science Foundation (NSF) were also expressing their concerns "about the growing shortage" of scientists and engineers (Burgess & Borrowman, 1969, p. 124).

Reform meant returning to educational practices and requirements critics believed to have existed before the Great Depression, the subsequent entry of first-generation high school students, and the introduction of life-adjustment education. After *Sputnik* the focus was not on those students who a few decades earlier would not have been in high school but on preparing talented students—the gifted—in the academic disciplines, especially mathematics and science, so they could advance to college and master advanced disciplines that were relevant to the nation's defense needs.

The National Defense Education Act. In January 1958, President Eisenhower asked Congress to appropriate funds for the improvement of the nation's public schools. He asked not for the general aid that was then urged by William G. Carr the executive secretary of the National Education Association but recommended categorical aid—a series of measures directly related to the nation's defense requirements. He requested a 500 percent funding increase to enable NSF to continue work it had already begun to fund on the development of new mathematics and science curricula. He requested funds to enable the states to develop and strengthen their school guidance programs that Conant had urged as early as 1948 (Conant, 1948, p. 228). The purpose of the guidance programs was neither to assist students with their personal problems nor to help students identify their interests but to identify through the use of appropriate tests the talented students who were capable of studying a high school curriculum that would prepare them for admission to college. He asked for funds to support the improvement of foreign language instruction. He asked for funds to enable the public schools to purchase scientific equipment and materials for their laboratories and to hire additional science and mathematics teachers. To encourage more students to accept college teaching as a career he asked for funds for graduate fellowships.

Congress agreed with President Eisenhower's suggestion that plans to support school construction—a proposal he made in his 1952 presidential campaign—be deferred and passed the National Defense Education Act (NDEA). Its enactment demonstrated that while the political climate did not allow federal support for "general purpose aid" that public school officials wanted, it was possible to enact "special-purpose aid" or categorical aid. Provision of only categorical aid provided "a considerable measure of the very control" that opponents to federal aid to education wanted to avoid (Sundquist, 1968, p. 218). Through the NDEA the United States Office of Education was empowered to introduce NSF programs to the nation's schools. It had funds to improve instruction in science, mathematics and foreign languages. It also had funds to enable states to introduce guidance programs in their public schools and to fund programs in universities to train guidance counselors. It was able to encourage students to prepare for careers in mathematics, science, engineering, foreign languages or teaching through a student-loan program. NDEA also authorized funds to encourage studies in anthropology, economics, geography, history and political science so that the United States would be able to develop intelligence about those areas of the world where it was competing with the Soviet Union for power and influence. The support NDEA provided public school systems for the purchase of materials and equipment for their science and mathematics curricula and for the employment of supervisors of those curricula complemented the work that the National Science Foundation began to support in 1956, a year before *Sputnik,* when it began its sponsorship of the Physical Science Study Committee (PSSC).

The New Physics and the New Math. Massachusetts Institute of Technology physicist Jerrold Zacharias and other physicists believed that a new physics curriculum that placed more emphasis on basic ideas and less emphasis on practical applications would attract more students to the study of physics. The new physics was to give less attention to the classical physics of Newton and to emphasize nuclear physics. Rather than being drilled in Newton's laws and their applications students were to study nuclear physics and learn about particle physics. To facilitate the introduction of the new physics into the public schools Zacharias proposed the production of ninety twenty-minute movies. Teachers were then expected to use the questions, problems, and equipment that was to be produced to accompany the films

After *Sputnik,* the PSSC was awarded millions of dollars annually from NSF and from private foundations to produce the new physics. The PSSC organized summer workshops to produce the new materials and even a new textbook for the new course. Other workshops were organized to train teachers to teach the new course. By 1960, materials for the new physics had been tested in five hundred schools, and the new physics was declared ready for use in the nation's schools. Public school systems used NDEA funds to purchase the materials and equipment the new course required. The federal government had not ordered the public schools to teach the new physics. It did, however, support a sector of the scientific community that believed a new course was necessary and supported school systems that wanted to adopt the new course. For many public school officials it was easier to adopt the new course than to explain why it was not being adopted. The federal government was not exercising direct control of the public school curriculum, but it was, through funding, exercising its power to introduce changes.

The new math, like the new physics, antedated *Sputnik.* As early as 1919 the National Committee on Mathematical Requirements appointed by the Mathematical Association of America indicated the need for a revised approach to the mathematics curriculum. The Committee then recommended that formal demonstration should be preceded by informal and experimental work and that the emphasis on the manipulation of symbols should be seen as a way to improve speed and accuracy once understanding of basic principles had been achieved (Gage, 1963, pp. 1009–1010).

In 1952 Max Beberman of the College of Education at the University of Illinois and Herbert E. Vaughan of the University's Mathematics Department founded the University of Illinois Committee on School Mathematics (UICSM). The UICSM used the University's laboratory school as a site for development and testing of a new mathematics curriculum that focused on students' understanding of mathematical relationships. In place of teaching students how to use rules that produced correct answers but produced little or no understanding of mathematical relationships UICSM advocated instruction in set theory so students would learn how to relate mathematical concepts to each other.

In 1957, the University of Maryland began a Mathematics Project to determine the best way to teach mathematics to junior-high-school students. The Maryland Project created a curriculum that abandoned drilling of students in rules they did not comprehend and sought to teach students how to handle mathematical abstractions. In 1959, the Commission on Mathematics that had been appointed by the College Entrance Examination Board in 1955 reported that conventional teaching of mathematics not only failed to interest students in mathematics but also failed to teach an understanding of the subject.

In 1958 NSF awarded a grant to Edward G. Begle of Yale's Mathematics Department to organize the School Mathematics Study Group (SMSG) to develop an improved mathematics curriculum. The SMSG met in the summer of 1958 and decided that the most efficient way to change the teaching of mathematics was to write new textbooks for grades seven through twelve. When the public schools opened in the fall of 1959, SMSG had already prepared a series of texts for grades seven through twelve for use by more than 250,000 students. In the spring of 1960, SMSG began its revision of the elementary school mathematics curriculum. In the early 1960s, many parents who had agreed that the schools needed to be improved complained that they were unable to assist their children with their mathematics homework. Parents knew how to compute but did not know how to relate mathematical concepts to each other.

SMSG and PSSC were not the only groups that worked on new materials for the schools in the summer of 1959. As Jerome S. Bruner (1961) reported:

> A tour of the United States in the summer of 1959 would have revealed a concentration of distinguished mathematicians in Boulder, Colorado, engaged in writing new textbooks for primary, junior high, and high school grades. In Kansas City, there could be found a group of first-class biologists busily producing films on subjects such as the structure of the cell and photosynthesis for use in tenth-grade biology classes. In Urbana, Illinois, there was a flurry of work on the teaching of fundamental mathematical concepts to grade-school children, and in Palo Alto one might have found a mathematical logician at work trying out materials for teaching geometry to children in the beginning grades of school. In Cambridge, Massachusetts, work was progressing on an "ideal" physics course for high school students, engaging the efforts not only of text writers and film producers but also of men who had earned world renown in theoretical and experimental physics. At various centers throughout the country, teachers were being trained to teach this new physics course by others who had already tried it. Preliminary work was under way in Boulder on a junior high school course in biology, and a group of chemists were similarly engaged in their field in Portland, Oregon. (pp. vii–viii)

As Bruner reported, physics and mathematics were not the only subjects that scholars believed needed revision. In 1959, the American Institute of Biological Sciences Curriculum Study (BSCS) was founded to design a new biology curriculum. In 1960, the Chemical Educational Material Study Group (CHEM Study) began work on a new text, laboratory manuals, a teacher's guide, and movies for a new chemistry course. In 1962, the American Council of Learned Societies and Educational Services Incorporated worked to develop a comprehensive and unified structure that would allow the creation of new courses in the humanities and social sciences that would be analogous to those in the sciences and mathematics.

Historically, proposals for federal support for public education failed to overcome the resistance by one or more of what was then commonly known as the three Rs: Race, Religion, and Reds (Communism). Race was an issue because some members of Congress wanted to ensure that those schools that served mainly African-American students would be treated fairly and equally, and others invoked the doctrine of states' rights to ward off any regulations on how federal aid was to be used. Religion was an issue that was not easily resolved, for some in the Congress insisted upon aid to Catholic schools, and others objected to any such aid. Still others argued that federal support would entail federal regulation, that federal regulation would be a move toward totalitarianism, and totalitarianism was, of course, communism (Ravitch, 1983, pp. 5–6; Davies, 2007, pp. 9–11). Those arguments disappeared in *Sputnik's* wake. Traditional objections to federal involvement and support for public education became irrelevant as the United States Congress enacted the National Defense Education Act (Public Law 85-864), the primary purpose of which was to provide to all levels of education, public and private, to improve and expand education in science, mathematics, and foreign languages so the nation would have the knowledgeable human capital necessary for the nation's defense.

It had taken Congress and the president more than five years to agree on a bill to create the National Science Foundation, but *Sputnik* prompted quick action. In the opening paragraph of the National Defense Education Act Congress explained why it acted so promptly:

> The Congress hereby finds and declares that the security of the Nation requires the fullest development of the mental resources and technical skills of its young men and women. The present emergency demands that additional and more adequate opportunities be made available. The defense of this Nation depends upon the mastery of modern techniques developed from complex scientific principles. (reproduced in Krug, 1966, p. 140)

The Soviet Union's successful launching of *Sputnik I,* and then *Sputnik II,* constituted the "present emergency." That emergency required the production of an increased supply of knowledgeable human capital for the nation's defense. Under the guise of national defense, Congress provided funds that supported public education.

Foreign Language. That NDEA provided support for foreign language instruction as well as mathematics and science is not surprising, for Earl James McGrath, the United States Commissioner of Education, had earlier reported that between 1920 and 1940 the percent of high school students studying a foreign language fell from twenty-seven to fourteen. The role of the United States in international affairs at the end of World War II required that the trend of fewer students studying foreign language be reversed. Facility in foreign language helped to overcome the barriers and misunderstandings that sometimes existed between the United States and other nations. Maintaining the "good will" of nations "outside the Iron Curtain" was necessary for successful prosecution of the Cold War. The ability of the United States "to lead the Free World," he argued, "will be determined not only by the financial and other assistance we can give foreign countries in improving their lot, but more particularly in the attitudes of good will that we can inspire in them by showing that we respect and value their cultures and their ways of life." Knowing the language of a nation was the "gateway to the intellectual, the emotional, and the spiritual life of a nation" (McGrath, 1953, pp. 104–105).

At the beginning of the twenty-first century, as the United States embarked on a war against terrorism and as the nation considered its ability to compete on the global marketplace, enrollment in foreign language courses in public schools and on college campuses increased. The Modern Language Association reported that between 2002 and 2006 enrollment in foreign language courses increased by 12.9 percent. There were significant increases in the number of students studying Arabic. In that four-year period the number of students enrolling in Arabic courses increased from just over 10,000 to nearly 24,000. During the same period, the number of schools (two-year and four-year colleges) offering such courses reached 466, almost twice as many four years earlier ("Foreign Language Study Booming," 2007, p. 9).

The nation's desire to compete successfully on the global marketplace has apparently encouraged students to study Chinese. The American Council on the Teaching of Foreign Languages conducted a survey of foreign language enrollments and found that by 2007, there were more than 550 schools (K–12) offering courses in Chinese. It was then estimated that between 30,000 and 50,000 students were studying Chinese. The Modern Language Association reported that between 2002 and 2007 enrollment in college-level Chinese courses increased by 51 percent (Weise, 2007, p. 2A).

A Roper poll conducted near the end of 2004 showed that almost half of Americans believed that the nation's public schools did not offer enough instruction in foreign languages. By 2005 there was a growing recognition that: "To connect with peoples around the world—for trade, diplomacy, security, and scientific advancement—the United States needs individuals with skills in the world's diverse languages." Foreign languages were once again important. The nation had to make a significant investment in developing citizens' capabilities to compete with Europe. In Europe more than 50 percent of adults have full command of a second language, and in the United States about 9 percent of adults were able to make a similar claim (Christian, Pufahl, & Rhodes, 2005, pp. 226–227).

Educators Turn to the Disciplines. In the wake of *Sputnik*, scholars from a variety of academic disciplines were recruited to revise and update the public schools' curricula. In September 1959, thirty-five scientists, scholars, and educators met for ten days at Woods Hole on Cape Cod "to discuss how education in science might be improved in our primary and secondary schools" (Bruner, 1961, p. vii). The meeting was called by the Education Committee of the National Academy of Sciences and was financed by the National Science Foundation, the United States Office of Education, the United States Air Force, and the Rand Corporation. The assembled scholars believed that many significant advances made in the various disciplines during the previous half century had not yet reached the nation's elementary and secondary schools. They assembled to develop new curricula to remedy that situation and were meeting to explore ways to impart to students "a sense of the substance and method of science" (p. vii).

Bruner explained that as the enrollment in the American high school steadily increased during the twentieth century, it became increasingly difficult to maintain the proper balance "between instruction in the useful skills and in disciplined understanding." Conant's "plea for the comprehensive high school" was, Bruner maintained, an attempt to redress that imbalance (Bruner, 1961, p. 5). The Woods Hole Conference was an effort by the assembled scholars and scientists to redress the imbalance by considering "anew the nature of the learning process" (p. 2). The way to redress the imbalance and to improve the public schools' curricula was to emphasize the structure of the disciplines. Accordingly, the emphasis in his report of the conference was "principally on the intellectual side of education." Other educational considerations were not necessarily "less important" but it was then necessary to ask: "Are we producing enough scholars, scientists, poets, lawmakers, to meet the demands of our times?" (p. 9). It was necessary to maintain "a constant scrutiny of the 'fundamental character'" of what was taught in the elementary and the secondary schools in order to lessen the gap between the lower grades of public schools and the discoveries of the best scholars at the universities" (pp. 24–26).

According to Bruner (1961), the public school curriculum was to be organized neither by the interests of students nor the practical applications of knowledge but by "the most fundamental understanding that can be achieved of the underlying principles that give structure to that subject" (p. 31). To ensure that the "underlying structure" of a discipline was given proper emphasis, it was necessary "that the best mind in any particular discipline must be put to work on the task" (p. 19). Experts in the various subjects were, he maintained, the only ones qualified to determine the content of school subjects.

Bruner also wanted the style, or the attitude, of the scholars to be communicated to the students. He suggested that there might be "certain general attitudes or approaches toward science or literature that can be taught in earlier grades that would have considerable relevance for later learning." He speculated that: "the attitude that things are connected and not isolated is a case in point" (Bruner, 1961, p. 27). Students were to learn how the scholars in the various disciplines thought about their work. There was a body of literature "about the forms of sensibility that make for literary taste and vigor." Historians had written about how they approached their work, gathered information, made, and defended generalizations. Mathematicians even had a name for such considerations—"heuristics" (p. 27). The task was to determine "what attitudes or heuristic devices are most pervasive and useful" so that "rudimentary versions of them" could be taught to students in public schools, beginning in the elementary grades. That seemed an appropriate approach, for there was the belief among the Woods Hole participants "that there is a continuity between what a scholar does on the forefront of his discipline and what a child does in approaching it for the first time (p. 28).

The Woods Hole participants began with "the hypothesis that any subject can be taught effectively in some intellectually honest form to any child at any stage of development" (Bruner, 1961, p. 72). That hypothesis allowed the scholars to propose any subject matter they wished for the curriculum. Educators only needed to present the material in a form and manner consistent with the child's developmental stage. During each grade of school, or at each developmental stage, students would study the same subject. At each stage, or grade, however, the sophistication of the subjects taught would be increased as students progressed from one psychological stage to the next, from the stage of concrete operations to that of formal operations. Bruner (1961) further explained that the criterion for selection of material was simple:

> We might ask, as a criterion for any subject taught in primary school, whether, when fully developed, it is worth an adult's knowing, and whether having known it as a child makes a person a better adult. If the answer to both questions is negative or ambiguous, then the material is cluttering the curriculum. (p. 52)

Those questions were consistent with the belief that the purpose of the elementary school was to prepare students for high school, that the high school was to prepare students for college, and that college was to prepare students for professional careers or graduate school.

The Process of Education was widely noted, highly praised, and used to defend a variety of educational strategies. By 1971, it had been translated into twenty-one languages. The Soviets were the first to translate it. Educational reformers under Nikita Khrushchev believed it supported their claim that students had to be led to discover the virtues of "socialist realism" rather than have it presented to them. In Italy it was "used in a battle by the moderate Left, against doctrinaire Marxist educators on the one side and against traditionalists on the other who wanted to maintain a classical curriculum" (Bruner, 1977, p. 198). In the United States, Frank G. Jennings likened Bruner's efforts at synthesizing the views of the Woods

Hole participants to an "alchemist's efforts." Bruner, Jennings claimed, had "transmuted the inquiry of specialists into a declaration of the intellectual rights, duties, and desires of all who would teach and learn, not only in science but in the whole range of knowledge and experience" (Jennings, 1960, p. 94). G. J. Sullivan described Bruner's work as an "an epochal book" that provided "accurate expression to the current ferment in educational thought in the country." He further suggested that it would lay "to rest the ghosts of some outmoded approaches" and offered "an exciting discussion of the direction educational theory and research should now take" (Sullivan, 1961). While Paul Goodman suggested that Bruner did not fully "appreciate the moral and ideological obstacles that are put in the way of teaching children fundamental real ideas in the study of man," he nonetheless claimed it would be a classic "comparable for its philosophical centrality and humane concreteness to some of the essays of Dewey" (Goodman, 1960, p. 28).

After the Woods Hole Conference, educators conducted and attended conferences and seminars devoted to the disciplines. The National Education Association's Project on Instruction sponsored a Seminar on the Disciplines that "was called to facilitate study and use of the disciplines by (a) focusing upon those fundamental ideas and methods of inquiry from selected fields of study which should be in the mainstream of the instructional program of the public schools, and (b) exploring the frontier thinking and research in the nature of knowledge and ways of knowing" (*The Scholars Look at the Schools*, 1962, p. 2). Soon after the NEA seminar ended, the University of Wisconsin-Milwaukee School of Education used funds provided by the Uhrig Foundation to sponsor an invitational conference on "The Nature of Knowledge." The conference participants discussed the need for knowing, ways of knowing, knowledge and the structure of the disciplines, conceptions of knowledge and their significance for the school curriculum, knowledge about knowledge for teachers, the structure of knowledge and the interrelationships of ideas, and the relationships among knowledge, schooling and the preparation of teachers (Jenkins, 1961).

James Bryant Conant and the American High School

Conant who had been appointed president of Harvard University in 1933, because of his scientific accomplishments and administrative ability, became an important figure when World War II began. In 1940 he joined the National Defense Research Committee (NDRC) and was sent to England to work out ways to exchange scientific information between the two countries. When the Manhattan District was organized in June 1942 to administer the building of the first atomic bombs, Conant served as the scientific advisor to its director and was a member of the committee that advised President Truman on the use of the atomic bomb. He returned to Harvard in 1947. In 1953 President Eisenhower named him High Commissioner to the new West German Government in Bonn. When West Germany was granted its autonomy in 1955, he was appointed the United States Ambassador to the new nation.

As president of Harvard, Conant sought to persuade the faculty in the School of Education "that the study of education as a social process—quite apart from the training of teachers—is as important as the study of law or of business administration" (quoted in Powell, 1980, p. 213). Conant's "conception of education as a social process matured during 1939 as he grew more sensitive to threats against the American political and economic system" (p. 213). He believed the American high school could be used to sustain the democratic system of government. It was the one institution where all youth could not only be taught the principles of democracy but also offered an opportunity for social mobility. His interest in the relationship among education, social mobility, and social stratification continued after World War II ended. He believed that public education "could unify an excessively diverse and stratified society" but feared that schools "were often a barrier to mobility." According to Arthur G. Powell, "social science studies such as Lloyd Warner's *Who Shall Be Educated?* (1944) confirmed his suspicion that the schools were not an independent force for mobility and equality of opportunity but were entangled with the social structure as a whole" (p. 232).

In February 1957, about eight months before the launch of *Sputnik I*, Conant returned to the United States to begin a study of the nation's public schools. His study was funded by the Carnegie Corporation and administered by the Educational Testing Service.[3] The schools Conant and his associates visited "were located for the most part outside metropolitan areas in cities with populations between 10,000 and 100,000" (Conant, 1959a, p. 14). They visited schools in twenty-six states, avoiding the South except for Kentucky, Maryland, and Virginia. Conant's team visited four school systems and 103 schools. Conant visited three school systems and fifty-five schools. The schools he accounted for in *The American High School Today* enrolled about 30 percent of the nation's high school students. These were suburban highs schools that he had earlier described as "the pride of our public school system." They were located in "well-to-do" communities where taxes where sufficient to provide the support they needed for "a homogeneity of population" (p. 46).

In *The American High School Today*, Conant did not compare the nation's schools to those of other nations. He maintained that the schools in the United States were rooted in a different social, economic, and political tradition from those in other nations. The American comprehensive high school was an invention of Americans in the twentieth century. No other nation had a comparable institution, and it was to be found in nearly all communities. There was only one major question to ask:

> Can a school at one and the same time provide a good general education for *all* the pupils as future citizens of a democracy, provide elective programs for the majority to develop useful skills and educate adequately those with a talent for handling advanced academic subjects—particularly foreign languages and advanced mathematics? (Conant, 1959a, p. 15)

An affirmative answer to that question was necessary to ensure the nation's security and its future. An affirmative answer meant that: "no radical change in the basic pattern of American education would seem to be required" (p. 15). Conant believed it was possible for most, if not all, communities to have a comprehensive high school. If a high school were large enough to have a graduating class of one hundred students, the school would be able to offer all the courses all the students needed at a reasonable cost.

So that "interested citizens" could determine how good their high schools were, Conant provided the checklist he developed for this survey. His fifteen-item checklist, divided into four major sections, was considerably less complicated than the sixty-three-item instrument the editors of *Life* earlier prepared to assist its readers in determining how good their schools were ("How Good is Your School," 1950, pp. 54–55). The first section of Conant's checklist was devoted to "general education for all." It focused on the school's program in composition and literature (American and English), social studies, and history, and asked whether students were grouped according to their abilities in the required courses. The second section addressed questions about the "non-academic elective program." An appropriate program provided "vocational programs for boys and commercial programs for girls," offered "opportunities for supervised work experience," and made "special provisions for very slow readers." The third section focused on the program for the "academically talented students." For those students the good high school was to have programs that challenged the gifted, such as "special instruction in developing reading skills," summer sessions for enrichment, and "individualized programs" characterized by an "absence of tracks or rigid programs." The fourth section asked about the school's guidance program, student morale, the organization of homerooms, and "effective social interaction." Schools, according to Conant, had an obligation to address the diversity of students' interests and backgrounds. They were to foster "understanding between students with widely different academic abilities and vocational goals" (Conant, 1959a, pp. 19–20). That "understanding" was to be accompanied through "well-organized homerooms and certain student activities" and through a senior-level course in American problems or American government in which students would be "heterogeneously grouped" (p. 75).

Conant reported that he tried to give each school he visited a simple yes-or-no answer for each question. Presumably, interested citizens could visit their schools and do the same. He paid special attention to the teaching of mathematics, science, and foreign languages. He found that school officials were not able to report with any certainty how many of the academically talented seniors enrolled in physics, senior mathematics, and a foreign language course. He asked twenty-two principals to prepare an "academic inventory" for him, showing what courses the top 25 percent of the senior class had taken during their stay in high school. Those inventories showed that there were only eight schools "satisfactorily fulfilling the three main objectives of a comprehensive high school." The schools were not offering a sufficiently wide rage of academic courses, and "the majority of the bright boys and girls were not working hard enough" (1959a, pp. 22–23). The schools were not doing what they needed to do to produce a sufficient supply of knowledgeable human capital for the nation.

Conant urged school boards to adopt policies that would require academically talented high school students to complete an eighteen-course program, consisting of four years of mathematics, four years of one foreign language, three years of science, four years of English, and three years of social studies. Students enrolled in that program were also expected to do three hours of homework. In addition, he recommended that provision should be made for the academically talented students to take additional courses in social studies and foreign language.

Conant explained that the policies he recommended were policies that, if implemented, would create increased opportunities for individuals:

> From the point of view of the individual, failure to develop talent in school may be the equivalent of locking many doors. For example, without mathematics and science in high school, it would be difficult to enter an engineering school, to take a premedical course in college, and impossible to begin a scientific career in a university. (Conant, 1959a, p. 59)

The neglect of "the 15 percent of the youth who are academically talented" also had social consequences. It meant either a diminution of the pool from which "professional men and women" could be drawn or a group of professionals who were not as well prepared for their responsibilities as they should be.

Conant believed that "academically talented youth ought to elect a full program of stiff courses in high school and ought to go to college," but deliberately avoided describing his recommended program as a "college-preparatory program" (1959a, p. 60). Variations in admission requirements and courses of study in the nation's colleges and universities made it impossible to attach that label to any one program. However, to many parents and many educators his recommendations appeared to be a restatement of what for years had been the traditional college-preparatory curriculum recommended by the Committee of Ten in 1893. For example, Richard Hofstadter observed that there was a "close similarity" between Conant's program and that recommended by Charles W. Eliot and the Committee of Ten (Hofstadter, 1963, p. 330).

Conant's recommendations for the high school were widely noticed and generally received favorable review from the mass media. For example, Fred M. Hechinger wrote in *The New York Times* that Conant "successfully avoids arousing the opposition to a sham war of words" and described him as a "peaceful reformer" who was supplied with "a battery of well-aimed facts" that had "great power to improve education" (Hechinger, 1959, p. 6).

In 1948, Conant argued that the nation's "success as a free people . . . in the 'cold war' with the Soviet Union" depended as much on the nation's "tax-supported schools" as the nation's success in World War II depended on "certain physicists and chemists" (Conant, 1948, pp. 36–37). In 1959, in *The Child, the Parent and the State* Conant drew attention to Premier Nikita Khrushchev's Memorandum of September 21, 1958 and pointed out that "Khrushchev boasts of the expansion of the educational system and attributes the successes in all branches of the national economy to the fact that Soviet schools have been able 'to train skilled personnel capable of tackling the most complex and responsible tasks'" (Conant, 1959b, p. 7). Conant then complained about educators who were "behind the times." Those educators, he claimed, "tend to resent any references to the struggle between free nations and Communism and the consequent existence of a special national interest which ought to affect educational planning" (p. 39). Educators had been so concerned with "the unfolding of the individuality of each child" that they were unable to recognize "that a new national concern might be an important factor which should be considered by a parent and a student in planning a high school program" (p. 40).

In a review of *The Child, the Parent and the State*, J. H. Stack wrote in *Chemical and Engineering News* that Conant had "offered 21 specific recommendations which are being used by many of our 21,000 public high schools to check their own quality" (Stack, 1960). W. H. Cornog observed in *The Chicago Sunday Tribune* that Conant had demonstrated that "the structure of American secondary education needs little in the way of major revision or reform" (Cornog, 1959, p. 6). Christopher Jencks objected to the attention Conant gave to the Soviets, rockets, engineers, and the cold war. Conant, he maintained, did not acknowledge that "the present school system is needlessly depriving millions of Americans of the chance to live the good life" (Jencks, 1959).

Conant's Second Report. In 1960, Conant's "first report" was followed by *A Memorandum to School Boards: Recommendations for Education in the Junior High School Years* that was financed by a grant from the Carnegie Corporation of New York to the Educational Testing Service. He described *A Memorandum* as "my second report to interested citizens" (Conant, 1960, p. 3). Conant thought of the junior high school as consisting of grades, seven, eight, and nine. His review of the junior high school, however, revealed great diversity in how it was organized. He found:

> These grades are often found as the first years of a separate three-year junior high school in a 6–3–3 system; again as the last two years of an eight-year elementary school in an 8–4 system. In a 6–2–4 plan they constitute a junior high school in themselves, and often they are the first two grades in a six-year high school in a 6–6 system. Some school systems split the two grades into a 7–5 arrangement; others include grades 7–10 or 6–8 in junior high schools. (Conant, 1960, p. 13)

Conant offered no recommendation about how the junior high school should be organized but he did emphasize "that the place of grades 7, 8, and 9 in the organization of a school system is of less importance than the program provided for adolescent youth" (Conant, 1960, p. 22). Junior-high-school students were adolescents, and adolescence was a time of physical, social, and emotional changes. The junior-high-school years constituted the time of transition from a school that emphasized the child to one that emphasized subject matter. For Conant, "concern for the physical, social, and emotional development of boys and girls properly exists at all levels, but as they progress through the grades the role of organized knowledge becomes increasingly important" (p. 23).

The advice Conant gave to school boards about the junior high school curriculum was consistent with what he had advocated for the high school. Sixty to 70 percent of the instructional time should be devoted to English, social studies, mathematics, and science. Art, music, and physical education were appropriate for all children. While instruction in basic skills that began in the elementary school was appropriate, provided students would benefit from that instruction, it was also necessary to allow that capable "small fraction of pupils to begin algebra in grade eight and study of a foreign language on a conversational level in grade seven." "The reason for the early identification of very able pupils and the start of mathematics beyond arithmetic," he explained, "is that at least some of these pupils can complete a four-year sequence by the end of grade 11 and be ready for college-freshman mathematics in grade 12" (Conant, 1960, p. 23). Students in the junior high school, like those in the high school, were to have homework but less of it: one hour in grade seven and two hours in grade nine.

Conant wanted the junior high school to prepare students for the senior high school. Teachers in the junior high had to have the characteristics of both elementary school and senior high school teachers. They needed "an understanding of children" and "considerable knowledge in at least one subject-matter field" (Conant, 1960, p. 27). His advocacy of block-time teaching was not an endorsement of "core programs" that focused on "the problems of young adolescents" that involved "considerable teacher-pupil planning" (p. 33). Block-time teaching was "to enable one teacher to know his pupils well" and be "in a position to counsel pupils who have been accustomed to the personal and solicitous attention of an elementary school teacher." It was to "effect a smooth transition for the pupil from the self-contained classroom with one teacher in the elementary school to the departmentalized situation with many teaches in the secondary school" (p. 23).

Except for guidance classes that focused on vocational opportunities for students who were likely to drop out of school in grades nine or ten, Conant was "not enthusiastic about sequential, regularly scheduled, group guidance courses as presented in some schools" (Conant, p. 27). "Minor social crises" could be handled either by homeroom teachers or block-time teachers. Junior high schools needed guidance counselors to help students plan appropriate programs, administer tests to provide information on which to make appropriate decisions about students' programs, and to tend to the personal, social, and academic problems of students.

Like his recommendations for the high school, Conant's proposals for the junior high school called for no radical changes. As Conant (1960) related, "the recommendations in this report, like those in my first report, are purposely conservative" (p. 45). The purpose of the junior high school was to prepare students for the senior high. To realize that purpose increased communication between elementary school teachers and junior high school teachers was essential. To coordinate subject matter from one grade to the next curriculum coordinators were needed. The curriculum coordinators, Conant emphasized, "must be competent in the subject fields for which they are responsible" (p. 33).

A Third Report. In 1961, Conant published *Slums and Suburbs.* For this report, Conant and his staff visited those metropolitan areas that they did not visit for the first report. Conant described it as "a book of contrasts." The contrasts he found between slum schools and suburban schools—schools frequently no more than a twenty-minute drive from each other—were enormous. Conant estimated that a third of the nation's children attended school in large metropolitan areas but that not all those students attended prosperous suburban schools. In the schools he visited for the first report, he found a "sense of social and economic cohesion" (Conant, 1961, p. 5) not found in the nation's ten largest metropolitan areas. He had earlier described the nation's suburban high schools as "the pride of our public school system" (p. 46), but no such pride could be taken in inner-city schools. The differences between the slum schools and the suburban schools were "appalling" (p. 2). As he had earlier suggested, "all high schools do not automatically make for national equality of opportunity" (Conant, 1948, p. 46).

In his first report and in his second report, Conant assured readers that radical change was not necessary. In *Slums and Suburbs,* he tried to convince readers that immediate changes were needed in American schools and American society. He warned that "social dynamite" was building up in American cities:

> I have sought to create a set of anxious thoughts in the minds of the conscientious citizens who may read these pages and who, while living in the suburbs, may work in the city. To improve the work of the slum schools requires an improvement in the lives of the families who inhabit the slums, but without a drastic change in the employment prospects for urban Negro youth relatively little can be accomplished. (Conant, 1961, p. 147)

In the spring of 1959, almost a third of unemployed workers were under age twenty-five. For the entire labor force, one out of nineteen was unemployed, but one out of seven teenagers were unemployed. The unemployment rate for African American teenagers was even higher, 24.8

percent or nearly one out of four (Sundquist, 1968, p. 73). In the slums, approximately two-thirds of African American youth who dropped out of school were unemployed. Telling them to remain in school to increase their chances for securing gainful employment made little sense, for about half of those who completed high school were also unemployed. Conant warned that: "Communism feeds upon discontented, frustrated, unemployed people." He feared that "the fate of freedom in the world hangs very much in the balance." The words "freedom," "liberty," and "equality of opportunity" could have no meaning for the unemployed youth of the slums. Those youth could not be expected "to understand the relentless pressures of communism" (Conant, 1961, p. 34).

In the 1950s, Americans were told that they needed to improve their schools to protect themselves from external threats. In the 1960s they were also told that they needed to improve their schools to protect themselves from internal threats, from the "social dynamite" building up in the nation's cities. To defuse the "social dynamite," Conant proposed: "*that in a heavily urbanized and industrialized free society the educational experiences of youth should fit their subsequent employment*" (p. 40, Conant's emphasis). He called for "a smooth transition" from school to work even if a student dropped out of school as early as the tenth grade. He called for more vocational programs and more vocational guidance. He wanted schools to assume responsibility for job placement. Schools needed more guidance counselors, and they "*ought to be given the responsibility for following the post-high school careers of youth from the time they leave school until they are twenty-one*" (p. 41, Conant's emphasis).

Conant recognized that more job preparation would be pointless if the jobs did not exist. At the time, a bill was before Congress to create a Youth Employment Act. One proposed program was similar to the Civilian Conservation Corps of the Depression Era, but Conant questioned its relevance for urban youth. Other programs called for job training programs conducted by local employers, trade unions, and schools. Conant endorsed those programs but emphasized that they would help "only if a non-discriminatory provision is included and enforced" (Conant, 1961, p. 39). He wanted Congress to appropriate funds for 300,000 jobs for youth between the ages of sixteen and twenty-one. That was, certainly in retrospect, a curious solution, for jobs were becoming more dependent on schooling than ever before. A high school diploma was increasingly becoming a necessary qualification for employment. Employment opportunities were needed, but new conceptions of schooling were also needed to answer the challenges of the Post-World-War-II Era.

That Conant had different proposals for different populations—academic programs to prepare suburban youth for college and vocational programs supported by the federal government for inner-city youth—clearly indicated where he believed the talented youth were. Students' social-economic status, race, or ethnicity effectively determined the kind of school and the kind of program to which they were to have access. That recognition or recommendation was contrary to his earlier claim that the public high school needed to be configured to provide all individuals the opportunity for social mobility.

Poverty, the Civil Rights Act, and the Elementary and Secondary Education Act

In the 1960s, even before the United States demonstrated its scientific and technological capacities by landing a man on the moon,[4] eradication of poverty was moving up on the national agenda, and that meant a change of focus in education discourse. While educators were still attending conferences to discuss the importance and implications of the structure of knowledge for curriculum improvement and publishing new texts on curriculum that emphasized either the structure of knowledge (see, e.g., Phenix, 1964) or the possibility of having both democracy and excellence in education (see, e.g., Broudy, Smith, & Burnett, 1964), poverty was appearing on the national agenda. Children as opposed to adolescents were soon at the center of the nation's focus on poverty. The nation's concern about the welfare of children, especially those labeled as "disadvantaged," "was accompanied by an unprecedented expansion in government support of social service programs and social and behavioral science research in general and addressed to child development in particular" (Laosa, 1984, p. 40). Shortly after Michael Harrington published *The Other America* (1961) in which he introduced "the culture of poverty" and "the cycle of deprivation" to the nation's political and education discourse, President John F. Kennedy was asking what could be done about poverty (Watson, 2002, p. 520).

Soon after President's Kennedy's assassination, his successor Lyndon B. Johnson, declared an "unconditional wary on poverty" in his first State of the Union message on January 8, 1964. He subsequently announced his plans for the "Great Society" in a speech on May 22, 1964 at the University of Michigan. Congress supported his agenda and passed the Economic Opportunity Act (1964) that led to the establishment of Head Start (originally known as the Comprehensive Child Development Program), based on the premises and conclusions of research on children and youth in the interwar years. Congress then passed the 1964 Civil Rights Act and the Elementary and Secondary Education Act (ESEA) in1965. By the mid-1960s, education had a new mission. Public education was to put an end to poverty by providing new and enhanced educational opportunities for disadvantaged children. ESEA was enacted to address the lack of achievement among disadvantaged children, but the attention given to excellence and achievement was somehow not given the attention it should have been given. In the mid 1960s, the attention given to providing equality of educational opportunity by ending racial segregation in the nation's public schools tended to overshadow other initiatives and developments.

The 1964 Civil Rights Act. While 1950s' and early 1960s' education discourse largely focused on identifying talented youth, the *Brown* decision signified and inspired more than its simple ruling that racial segregation in public education was unequal and therefore unconstitutional. Those on the side of ending Jim Crow and extending civil rights and equality of opportunity to all Americans saw *Brown* as the opening of a new era. New organizations—for example, the Congress of Racial Equality and the Student Nonviolent Coordinating Committee—challenged Jim Crow laws and practices in public venues such as lunch counters in drug stores, five and dimes, department stores, and bus terminals. *Brown* marked the beginning of a renewed movement for ending racial discrimination that led to the Montgomery bus boycott in 1955 after Rosa Parks' arrest, the sit-ins at lunch counters that began in Greensboro, North Carolina in February1960, and "Freedom Rides" that began in May 1961. *Brown* and what it inspired served as the foundation for that phase of the civil rights movement that achieved passage of the 1964 Civil Rights Act, the most complex and comprehensive civil rights act ever passed by the United States Congress.

Title IV and Title VI of the 1964 Civil Rights Act are the two titles that proved to relate directly to how equality of educational opportunity was to be defined, measured, and implemented for the next decade. Title IV directed the United States Commissioner of Education to cause a survey to be conducted to determine whether equality of educational opportunity obtained in the United States and its territories. That led to *Equality of Educational Opportunity* now commonly known as *The Coleman Report.* Those who attended to the findings in *The Coleman Report* eventually had to acknowledge that there was more than one way to define or measure equality of educational opportunity and that some measures would receive more attention than others. That Congress ordered the report to be conducted indicates that there was good reason to believe that equality of educational opportunity, as measured by integration and thus by access to equally supported schools, was still not available to all the nation's children and youth.

Title VI specified that "No . . . person shall, on the grounds of race, color, or national origin be excluded from participation in, be denied the benefits of, or be subjected to discrimination under any program or activity receiving Federal financial assistance." Programs that had federal support and were found to be practicing discrimination were subject to having their federal funds withdrawn. Title VI may not have seemed important to public school officials when the Civil Rights Act was enacted in 1964. However, in 1965 when the United States Congress passed the Elementary and Secondary Education Act (ESEA). Title VI became important and useful for those who wanted to see implemented what *Brown* had earlier promised.

A Carrot and a Stick. Title I of ESEA served as a powerful carrot and Title VI of the Civil Rights Act served as a powerful stick for those school officials who were resisting desegregation of public schools. Title I of ESEA provided funds for school districts with disadvantaged students. It was the most important title, for most of the funds—nearly 80 percent of $1.2 billion—were in Title I. Most of the nation's school districts, especially those in urban areas, were eligible to receive ESEA funds. To qualify for ESEA funds school districts not only had to demonstrate that they served disadvantaged students—a requirement that was relatively easy to satisfy, especially for virtually all major urban school districts—but also had to demonstrate that they were complying with Title VI of the Civil Rights Act. That was more difficult for many districts because so many had failed to integrate their schools.

Title I as a carrot and Title VI as a stick did have some effect. Once Title I funds were available to virtually all school districts, some modest movement toward desegregation occurred. During the first year of Title I, "the proportion of black children attending school with whites rose from 2 percent to 6 percent, and 1,563 districts started to desegregate, more in a single year than in the preceding decade" (Wastson, 2002, p. 164). Many school districts, especially Deep-South districts, filed freedom-of-choice plans. Freedom-of-choice plans proved either to produce token integration or to maintain the existing racial segregation in the schools. For example, the United States Civil Rights Commission conducted a study and found 102 freedom-of-choice plans in which no African American students were attending school with white children (Ravitch, 1983, p. 164). Freedom-of-choice plans failed to end racial segregation in the schools because African Americans were often understandably often unwilling to face angry mobs protesting their attendance. They often had good reason to believe that local law officials would not protect them from protesting mobs. Boycotts, bomb threats, bombings, riots, near riots, or the presence of angry protesters when African American students registered, attempted to register, or actually enrolled in schools of their choice occurred in Alabama, Georgia, North Carolina, Kentucky, Tennessee, South Carolina, Maryland, and, of course, Little Rock where local and state resistance to school integration resulted in President Eisenhower's decision to send federal troops to enforce the order of a federal court that drew worldwide attention (Greenberg, 1994, p. 217).

Guidelines. he Department of Health, Education, and Welfare's Office of Education was assigned responsibility not only for the disbursement of ESEA Title I funds but also for the development of guidelines to determine whether school districts qualified for funds under the provisions of Title VI of the Civil Rights Act. The first guidelines, already developed by early April 1965, allowed school districts in which there was no segregation of either students or faculty to file an "assurance of compliance." Districts that were in the process of desegregating under court order were required to file a copy of the order, a report on how much segregation of students and faculty obtained, and a report on the progress being made toward desegregation. Other districts were permitted to submit a plan indicating how they would voluntarily desegregate their schools by the fall of 1967. Those districts were allowed to develop new compact attendance districts or to implement freedom-of-choice plans that allowed parents to choose the school they wanted their child to attend (Ravitch, 1983, p. 163).

To increase equality of educational opportunity (the rate of desegregation) the Office of Education revised its guidelines in March 1966. Besides all but disallowing freedom-of-choice plans, the new guidelines established "performance criteria"—some interpreted those criteria to mean quotas—for each school district for the 1966–67 school year. However the "performance criteria" were interpreted it was clear that it would be possible to measure the extent to which equality of educational opportunity—desegregation—was being achieved. School districts that had integrated 8 percent to 9 percent of its African American students into white schools were required to integrate 16 percent to 18 percent of its African American students into white schools. Districts that had adopted freedom-of-choice plans and that had failed to integrate any of its students were required to make a "very substantial start." According to the Office of Education, it was not sufficient for a school district to demonstrate that it was not practicing racial discrimination. School districts were now required to develop and to implement plans that would desegregate their schools. The Office of Education was clearly rejecting the "Briggs dictum." Equality of educational opportunity was to be measured by how many schools were desegregated and by how many students were or were not attending desegregated schools.

Subsequent to the signing of the 1964 Civil Rights Act, the federal courts began to call for an end to all delaying tactics and required more than token compliance with what *Brown* promised. The federal courts wanted to be able to measure how much integration was taking place. The courts held that freedom-of-choice plans were simply a way to avoid racial integration of public schools and that racial segregation in public schools was to be undone. In *United States and Stout v. Jefferson County Board of Education* (1966) Fifth Circuit Court Judge John Minor Wisdom expressed his dissatisfaction with plans that produced little or no desegregation. He indicated that the "patience of the Court" was being taxed and "the time has come for foot-dragging public school boards to move with celerity toward desegregation" (quoted in Greenberg, 1994, p. 382). He ordered the schools in Jefferson County to be racially balanced in a manner consistent with the recently published guidelines from the Office of Education. In *Green v. School Board of New Kent County* (1968), the Court ruled against freedom-of-choice plans that failed to produce desegregation. The Court wanted desegregation plans that would produce results that could be measured. In *Swann v. Charlotte-Mecklenburg Board of Education* (1971) the Court upheld the order of a federal district court that ordered the school district to undertake whatever action necessary to desegregate its schools. That was the decision that led to "school busing." It should be noted that so-called court-ordered bussing began not with *Brown* in 1954 but seventeen years after *Brown.*

Quality and Equality in Education

Nearly coincident with the appearance of *Equality of Educational Opportunity*, Princeton University's Council on Human Relations hosted a three-day conference on "Quality and Equality in Education." To explore how "a high quality education" could be provided for all students they invited twenty-four "schoolmen and academics of diverse viewpoints, disciplinary affiliations and experiences" to participate in the three-day conference. Ten were invited to present theme papers and fourteen were selected to discuss and respond to the theme papers (quoted in Greenberg, 1994, p. 382). In the Introduction to the conference proceedings the editors—Melvin M. Tumin and Marvin Bressler—indicated that during the previous decade's "Great Debate" over education neither equality nor quality received the attention each deserved. They addressed the major issues that dominated education discourse during the previous two decades and joined them in a way that few others had. The "critics," or the so-called enemies of public education, they maintained, were so concerned with "gifted children" that they "debased the concept of equality." The "educationists," the so-called friends of education, appeared not to be concerned with "intellectual rigor" and thus "violated the principle of quality" (Tumin & Bressler, 1966, p. 2).

Tumin and Bressler argued that there could be no equality without quality. Access to "*some* school" was "not [a] sufficient condition for 'equal educational opportunity'." Equality of educational opportunity did not then obtain because some students were "systematically handicapped by environmentally induced social and psychological deficits" and because some schools "dispense[d] high quality education exclusively to the academically gifted." The "inequities of a stratified society" disadvantaged all students, rich and poor. Schools "magnified the inequities" by providing "superior education" to some and "denying it to others." "Recent research," they claimed, showed that "the poor, Negroes, and Puerto Ricans" were among those who were denied access to superior education. At the other end of the social hierarchy, socially advantaged students whose abilities were average or below average often attended a school that measured its "success" by how many of its graduates were admitted to "prestige colleges." Students who attended those schools suffered unfavorable consequences as they were given the impression that they were failures when they were not admitted to one of the "prestige colleges." The class-based system of education worked against the welfare of the individual. Whether rich or poor, the result was that the "individual experience[d] a deflation of self, anxiety, and hostility." The class-based system of education that did not provide equal educational opportunity "severely restrict[ed] the positive functions of education as a mechanism for recruiting and discovering talent, as an agent for economic growth, as a vehicle for social mobility, and as an instrument for peaceable social change" (Tumin & Bressler, 1966, pp. 1–2).

In the essay—an essay they acknowledged as "partisan"—Tumin and Bressler provided at the end of the *Proceedings*, they claimed that the nation was "engaged in a revolutionary effort to provide free, public, and high quality education to all the young people of society regardless not only of the differences in race, religion, or national origin, but more important, *regardless of their differences in talent and ability*" (Tumin & Bressler, 1966, p. 1). Their claim was that all children were entitled to equal access to education for "an entire lifetime," for "no one ever knows enough to exploit fully the possibilities of his own life or to enrich the lives of his fellows." They believed their claim could be realized, for there was reason to believe "that free public education probably will be extended beyond the twelfth year for more young men and women than the number for whom such advanced education is now available" (pp. 4–5). Equal education for all "young men and women" was an imperative if the nation was to have the necessary "manpower for the mainsprings of our productive capacity" (p. 11). Education was "simultaneously an investment and an item of consumption," and "necessary for social and individual welfare." It contributed to "social stability" and to "personal fulfillment" (p. 38).

Above all, Tumin and Bressler (1966) were committed to the proposition "that the first task of a free society is to complete the process of providing equal opportunity for first-rate schooling for all persons regardless of race, color, or creed." That task was "properly at the very top of our agenda of educational needs" (p. 42). To complete that task it was necessary to accept "that all children are equally entitled to a high quality education and that it is inadmissible in any general sense to set upper limits on the proper amount of education." By joining "the doctrines of 'no upper limit' and 'equal treatment,' they were urging "a significant increase in both the absolute and relative levels of support for American education" (p. 39).

Tumin and Bressler (1966) were cognizant of "the fact that there exists in our population diverse nationality, religious, racial and class groups, and more problematic, perhaps than any other, there are great ranges of differences in natural capacities." The common school was charged with dealing all students "even-handedly," and it was necessary that it continue to do so and to prepare students for "peaceful and productive cultural pluralism (p. 14).

Tumin and Bressler (1966) wanted to assign "equal weight" to "equality and quality" and "to non-cognitive as well as cognitive aspects of education." They explained that:

> ...quality education aims not alone at refinement of cognitive capacities, though these are unavoidably part of such education, but at certain crucial psychological and social targets as well. For we believe that our schools must exhibit equal concern for the sensibilities as well as the minds of the students; for their understanding of themselves and their positions in society; and their senses of self-esteem; their capacity to relate easily and amiably to others who differ from them in background or capacity; their ability to manage their normally predictable life tasks and to participate in intelligent reconstruction of their society; and their derivation from their school experiences of a life-long and deep commitment to the value of schooling and to the democratic social institutions which make such education possible. (1966, p. 6)

Tumin and Bressler realized that there were obstacles in the way of providing equal quality education for all children. Among the obstacles were: claims that education had to be rationed in favor of those who were identified as gifted and thus needed to be educated to serve the national interest; the elite of the privileged classes who wanted to maintain their advantages for the benefit of their children; an emphasis on those designated as gifted or talented at the expense of those not so designated; stereotyping; the use of testing, grading, and tracking in the nation's schools; and common definitions of quality in education.

The National Interest. Tumin and Bressler (1966) rejected the argument that what the nation needed to prosecute the Cold War or what it needed to win the space race justified not providing all children with an equal quality education. They explained that:

> The most persuasive arguments against the full implementation of equal, quality education are advanced by those who assert the claims of the "national interest" against all other considerations. This orientation is informed by the requirements of cold war and intimations of hot war. Its proponents are especially sensitive to the need for a sophisticated technology that can only be developed by investing disproportionate amounts of our educational resources on training the youth who are talented in science, mathematics, and in allied applied disciplines such as engineering. (p. 18)

They acknowledged that there were crises—for example, World War II—that justified temporary departures from democratic processes, but did not see the Cold War as one of those crises. They maintained that:

> The demands of national security do not now seem to require any crash efforts in the field of science. Indeed, there is considerable doubt that the United States has ever lacked sufficient scientific and technical personnel in the area of defense. The grizzly word "overkill" summarizes our capacity to retaliate against any conceivable enemy. Similarly the space program has had recourse to an abundance of talent and even if this were not the case the prestige of making the first moon landing would not, in our judgment, justify any retreat from the principle that all children are entitled to an equally good education. (Tumin & Bressler, 1966, p. 19)

Privileged Classes. Those who vigorously opposed equal education were those who found "themselves and their children in relatively advantaged positions." They feared any social change or any educational measure that they saw as impairing "the educational and vocational careers of their children" (Tumin & Bressler, 1966, p. 19). That "quality education" was identified "with the welfare of the elite," Tumin and Bressler claimed, demonstrated "the disproportionate influence which high-status parents have been able to exert on the public school system of the United States" (p. 21). In place of giving the elite special considerations, they proposed "a very simple contrary ideal—namely that the schools of the United States should be operated for the equal benefit of all children" (p. 21). They maintained that the talent of each child merited full development.

Tumin and Bressler (1966) argued that no one political side—right or left—was better than the other when it came to fashioning arguments against providing equally good education for all children. Each side was on the side of denying education to minorities or the less fortunate in society. They maintained that:

> ... the educational right and left wings have joined in unwitting conspiracy to deny significant sectors of the population—the dull middle class, Negroes, Puerto Ricans, rural youth, urban migrants—the full advantages of serious training in the development of cognitive skills. Elitists disparage the intellects of those groups on the grounds of genetic insufficiency; liberal sentimentalists arrive at the same position because a cruel society has allegedly robbed large numbers of the ability to learn. Children are victimized by condescension whether its source is contempt or pity, for at bottom these are the same. (p. 7)

Such views had the potential to persuade teachers that not all children could be successful, and teachers who were so persuaded were not likely to develop ways to be successful with all children.

The Gifted. According to Tumin and Bressler (1966), those who developed arguments to defend denying or limiting the amount of education to some and granting more to others—the talented or the gifted, were finding ways to discriminate against minorities. They explained that:

> One version implicitly questions the entitlement of all persons to the best of society's resources. In its mild form this view assumes that those who are most able to benefit from social rewards deserve them. A more extreme extension of this argument postulates a natural order of superior and inferior human beings, some of whom "rate" a greater share of the world's goods and services. A familiar illustration of this approach is found among those who would deny first-class citizenship to Negroes and other minority groups. (p. 17)

To argue that some were more deserving of education than others was to argue for a return of feudalism: They explained that:

> We hold the idea that "superior" children are entitled to more education is a carry-over from a feudal mode of thought and practice in which differential advantages were the entitlement of the "well-born." Today's claim for different entitlement on the basis of talent or capacity is a counterpart of such a doctrine, insofar as it holds that those children who have good fortune to inherit superior "genes" should also have greater educational opportunities. This doctrine simply substitutes a modern aristocracy of genes for a feudal aristocracy of family. (p. 3)

Providing "special privileges" for gifted children was not to be confused with "quality education." No matter what a child's talent for academic work was, it had to be recognized that that child "has special needs, as special as those of any other" (p. 19).

Stereotyping. Tumin and Bressler (1966) wanted each child to be seen and to be treated not as a member of a group but as an individual. They objected to the assumptions that were made about children when they were not seen as individuals:

> We refer here to the widespread tendency to categorize pupils into major clusters or types, and to respond to these clusters in terms of certain assumed common characteristics of all so classified. Among the leading stereotypes are those which refer to the racial group of the child, the socio-economic class of his parents, and the label of his native ability. If pupils are seen primarily as Negro or white, they are not seen as individuals. If they are perceived primarily as lower or middle or upper class, they are not seen as individuals. If they are viewed primarily as fast or slow, smart or stupid by nature, their individual, variable profiles of capacity, over time, and for various kinds of performances simply cannot emerge clearly and be utilized sensitively. (pp. 27–28)

Any treatment of students based on their assignment to any given group was contrary to how teachers were expected to exercise their responsibilities. They maintained that:

> ... both law and custom charge the teacher with conducting the business of education as though racial, religious, nationality, ethnic and other diversities were irrelevant. None of these group identities which the child brings with him are to be allowed to become part of his effective school identity in any way that might interfere with his securing equal and equally appropriate relationships with his teachers and the curriculum. (pp. 14–15)

Testing. Tumin and Bressler (1966) were clearly opposed to standardized tests and to the use of intelligence tests to "cluster" students, for the effects on students and teachers worked against fair and equal treatment of students. They claimed that:

> Teachers are facilitated, perhaps unwittingly, perhaps purposely at times, in their tendency to stereotype students and to cluster them for mass treatment, by the endless round of testing of "abilities" and "achievements" that the schools sponsor and demand. Ability tests and instruments that measure I.Q.'s are equally culpable in this respect. (pp. 28–29)

The practice of using tests of students' abilities worked against the "possibilities of individuation, and in turn of equality and quality education" (p. 29). Moreover, they saw intelligence not as a fixed power that could be found with a testing instrument but as a product of education. They saw "intelligence as being *created* by the schools, and hence looks forward to much more intense interventions by the schools in all those aspects of a student's life—his family, his motivation, and the like—which are deemed relevant to his ability to succeed in school." It was the "weak version of equality" that advocated the early sorting of children into clusters (pp. 23–24).

Grading. Tumin and Bressler (1966) maintained that assignment of grades that indicated either success or failure reflected the imposition of "artificial, meaningless, uniform standards upon a widely variable school population" (p. 32). "To achieve equal, quality education for all" it was necessary to abandon "competitive marks, the graded curriculum and the concepts of pass and fail" (p. 34). They insisted that "assigning grades, such as A, B, C, or 100, 90, 80, etc. is both meaningless and harmful to sound education that presumes to be both equal and a level of high quality for all children" (p. 31).

Tracking. Tumin and Bressler (1966) clearly opposed tracking in the schools. Once a student was assigned to a track, it was not likely that he or she would be moved out of the track to which he or she was initially assigned. They claimed that: "No school on record is able to claim that as many as ten per cent of its student assigned to ability groups at the seventh or eighth grade levels move either up or down out of the groups of their initial assignment." Thus, schools needed to reexamine their tracking practices. Assignment of children to any group other than the "most favored," they claimed, demoralized them, "thereby further 'confirming' the validity of the initial assignment" (p. 29). To segregate children "on the basis of native intelligence or academic achievement" was, they claimed, "incompatible with any reasonable definition of quality and equality in education." In place of tracking they wanted heterogeneous grouping, for heterogeneous grouping had the potential for being "a positive asset to instruction" (p. 30).

Quality Education Defined. Tumin and Bressler (1966) rejected the notion that "the demand for special privileges for the gifted" was to "be equated with quality education" (p. 19). They objected to the tendency "to measure the 'quality' of a school by the proportion of the children who exceed national norms on various ability tests, enter college, secure outstanding scholarships, or in a very refined twist, enroll in universities that have Phi Beta Kappa chapters." Those who so defined quality education were to be found "in prosperous suburban communities with a high percentage of college-educated persons" (p. 20). That "quality education" was so defined and identified "with the welfare of the elite is striking evidence both of the disproportionate influence which high-status parents have been able to exert on the public school system of the United States" (p. 21).

Social Inequality and Social Change. Tumin and Bressler (1966) were very much aware of the inequalities in American society, how the social context in which schools operated affected their ability to function effectively, and how the social context affected students' "ability to develop their cognitive capacities to their fullest" (p. 6). They wanted students to be aware of that social context and to understand how society worked—how it was structured to advantage some and disadvantage others:

> It is important for students of all social strata to recognize the extent to which the "luck of the draw" or "accident of birth" gives some young people very decided advantages over others in crucial aspects of their social fates. The perception that the social environment provides resources and sets limits upon possible achievements discourages the self-congratulation of the advantaged and is one of the few possible sources of redemption from the burden of personal guilt that we are encouraged to assume for many of our shortcomings. Moreover, a realistic understanding of the actual operation of society would make it possible for young people to focus both on inequitable features of society as well as its main strengths. Thus prepared, they might become instruments for beneficent social change. (p. 13)

If students were to understand the operation of society, educators had to find ways to expand the curriculum so students would learn more than the then recent emphasis on the new mathematics and the new sciences. If the natural world was important, they argued, so was the social world. Students were, they maintained, surely capable of "grasping principles of sociology, anthropology, and economics." If schools were to provide quality education, they would accept the "responsibility for helping children to acquire an increasing grasp and deepening understanding of *all* their important worlds: those of physical nature, social and cultural systems, and humanistic and historical processes and products" (p. 8).

While Tumin and Bressler (1966) wanted students to be prepared to effect social change, they also wanted schools to be agencies for social change and to prepare students for new trends:

> No other institution has such a deeply vested, albeit nominal, interest in the exercise of critical reflection and in the adjustment of the very basic modes

> of its conduct to new trends in civilization. If a family chooses to stand on a tradition established by a remote ancestor, that is its option. If a corporation insists on maintaining certain principles of operation that are outmoded, the probable loss is, in theory, sustained only by the corporation, and it is not our official public concern. If churches persist in adhering to creeds and doctrines appropriate only to other centuries that is their right, however much we may dislike those doctrines. But if schools do not constantly adjust and readjust their curricula, methods, and administrative organizations to accommodate new developments in politics, science, art, morality, and international relations, then we hold this to be a matter of public concern requiring our attention. (p. 10)

If students were to be equipped to be "effective agents of social change, schools had the responsibility to teach "the habits and skills of social criticism" so those skills could be applied to the "deficiencies" not only of their own society but also "those of competing social systems" (p. 10).

Disadvantaged Students. Tumin and Bressler 1966) were clearly very much concerned with those students who were reared in impoverished circumstances that served to deprive them of equal educational opportunity. They maintained that:

> It is imperative also that we find the means to rescue children from the psychological assault and emotional deprivation that afflicts many of them even before they enter school.... It is clear that any child who is reared in an impoverished family environment, who has been taught in a thousand subtle ways that he is inferior, and who even as he starts school already lags behind others in cognitive skills is not likely to realize his full potential as a student and human being. (p. 41)

To not provide equal educational opportunity for all children, including those from impoverished families, was to risk costs or penalties that the nation certainly wanted to avoid. The ideals that American society consistently affirmed were "always under danger of erosion from the inequalities in opportunities and situations experienced by significant percentages of our people." That the nation's underprivileged had not "ever sought solutions for themselves or their fellow men outside the institutional boundaries of our society" was, they observed, "fortunate" (p. 45).

Notes

1. To hear the signals *Sputnik* sent back visit NASA's Website: http://nasa.gov/Sputnik.

2. That the federal government was concerned with the Soviet Union's education plans and capability is evidenced by publication of the U.S. Office of Education's Division of International Education, International Educational Relations Branch: *Education in the USSR* (Washington, DC, 1957) that appeared in May 1957, five months before the Soviet Union launched *Sputnik*.
3. When ETS opened for business on January 1, 1948 with Henry Chauncy as its president, Conant was its chairman of the board.
4. Apollo astronauts Neil Armstrong and Edwin Aldrin landed on the moon on July 20, 1969.

6

Equality of Educational Opportunity—The Coleman Report

Introduction

The 1964 Civil Rights Act and the 1965 Elementary and Secondary Education Act addressed the nation's recent "discovery" of poverty. *The Coleman Report*, a study conducted to satisfy a requirement of the 1964 Civil Rights Act, was the most comprehensive study of American education every taken. It clearly documented what is now known as "the achievement gap" between students from privileged communities and those from underprivileged communities and those classified as minority students.

Attention was directed to addressing the effects of poverty on student achievement and finding ways to overcome those effects. At the same time, some were clearly objecting to the attention that had been directed to identifying and cultivating talented or gifted students. Some responded to the attention directed to those who did not enjoy true equality of educational opportunity by looking for alternatives to traditional public education. Some sought alternatives within the public school system, and others

Equality of Educational Opportunity and Knowledgeable Human Capital, pages 107–125

looked outside the system. Still, others sought to improve public education by calling for accountability.

Equality of Educational Opportunity and Academic Achievement

To determine whether equality of educational opportunity was available to all the nations' children and youth the United States Commissioner of Education was ordered by Title IV, Section 402 of the Civil Rights Act "to conduct a survey and make a report to the President and the Congress, within two years... concerning the lack of availability of equal educational opportunities for individuals by reason of race, color, religion, or national origin in public educational institutions at all levels in the United States, its territories and possessions, and the District of Columbia" (Coleman et al., 1966, p. iii).

Alex M. Mood, the Assistant Commissioner for Educational Statistics, assigned the task of conducting the survey to James S. Coleman from Johns Hopkins University and Ernest Q. Campbell from Vanderbilt University. Mood agreed that the researchers could collect data that would allow them to investigate the relationships among students' family backgrounds, schools' resources, and students' academic achievement (Cohen & Barnes, 1999, p. 23). *Equality of Educational Opportunity* (commonly known as the *Coleman Report*) and the analyses and criticism to which it was subjected not only ensured that the need to extend equality of educational opportunity to all the nations' children and youth would remain high on the national agenda but also made clear that there was more than one way to define and measure equality of educational opportunity.

The Coleman Report is arguably the most-well known and the most comprehensive study of American education ever conducted. The $1.5 million the researchers had at their disposal enabled them to collect data from 570,000 students, 60,000 teachers, and 4,000 elementary and secondary schools. The Educational Testing Service (ETS) administered standardized tests to students, and James S. Coleman and his associates analyzed the data. Notwithstanding the cost and the magnitude of the study, its release was initially met with "deafening silence." In part that may have been because it was released just before the weekend of July 4, 1966. In part that may have been because the project's advisory panel "refused to sign off on it, citing methodological concerns." Subsequently, others would express methodological concerns and there soon developed a cottage industry devoted to questioning, examining, and analyzing the measurements, methods, and the conclusions of *The Coleman Report* (see, e.g., Spady, 1973, pp. 135–137).

That "the experience of statisticians that when fairly "crude" measurements are refined, the change more often than not turns out to be small" (Mosteller & Moynihan, 1972, p. 13) was generally not considered by the critics.

The Coleman Report received and continued to receive attention. As indicated by the claim in the June 21, 2006 issue of *Education Week, The Coleman Report's* "influence" was still "felt 40 years later." Perhaps the first significant attention given *The Coleman Report* was that given by Christopher Jencks in October 1966. For Jencks (1966), it was "the most important piece of educational research in recent years" (p. 21). The title of Jencks' review—"Education: The Racial Gap"—was significant and certainly not misleading, for *The Coleman Report* clearly demonstrated that members of minority groups tended not to perform as well in school as their majority-group counterparts.

Coleman and his associates examined the educational opportunities available to six racial and ethnic groups: "Negroes, American Indians, Oriental Americans, Puerto Ricans living in the continental United States, Mexican Americans, and whites other than Mexican Americans and Puerto Ricans often called 'majority' or simply 'white" (Coleman et al., 1966, p. iii). They collected data to answer questions in four areas:

1. They attempted to determine how much segregation existed among the various racial and ethnic groups in the nation's public schools. Integration was, according to the Supreme Court, a measure of equality of educational opportunity, and thus segregation was a measure of inequality of educational opportunity.
2. They attempted to determine whether all public schools offered equal educational opportunity by colleting information on laboratory facilities; textbooks; libraries; curricula; teacher characteristics, such as training and education, experience, salaries, attitudes and verbal ability; and several student characteristics, such as socioeconomic status, parents' education, academic goals and other attitudinal measures. To determine whether all students had access to schools that had equal resources was still another way to determine or measure whether equality of educational opportunity existed.
3. They measured student learning, or academic achievement, by examining students' performances on standardized tests. Early in the twenty-first century, when No Child Left Behind (NCLB) was enacted, the ability to predict students' achievement based on their membership in a racial, ethnic, or socialeconomic group became an important, if not the most important, consideration in measuring equality of educational opportunity.

4. They tried to determine whether student achievement was related to the characteristics of the schools students attended. That was essentially an attempt to determine whether schools made a difference in how well students performed on achievement tests. NCLB would later maintain that schools could make a difference and thus were required to do so.

Before *Equality of Educational Opportunity* was completed Coleman predicted that the survey would reveal "striking" differences between schools attended by African Americans and those attended by whites. He predicted that:

> . . . the study will show the difference in the quality of schools that the average Negro child and the average white child are exposed to. You know yourself that the difference is going to be striking. And even though everybody knows there is a lot of difference between suburban and inner city schools, once the statistics are there in black and white, they will have a lot more impact. (quoted in Mosteller & Moynihan, 1972, p. 8)

When Coleman and his associates began their study, they were effectively accepting a measure of equality of educational opportunity determined by inputs or resources. If, for example, the facilities, materials, teachers, and per pupil expenditures between and among schools were equal, then, according to this measure, equality of educational opportunity obtained. They expected to find great differences in the schools attended by African American students and the schools attended by white students but they did not find what they expected to find. They also accepted segregation as a measure of equality of educational opportunity.

The Coleman Report established that a decade after the Supreme Court ruled that "separate but equal" was not equal and therefore unconstitutional, the nation's schools were still mostly racially segregated. Therefore, inequality obtained, for the Supreme Court had created a measure of equality of educational opportunity that was related neither to resources or input nor to student performance, or output. Segregated schools were not and could not be equal. If the measure of educational equality was integration, then in the mid-1960s inequality persisted, for Coleman found that most of the nation's children were still attending racially segregated schools. Nearly two thirds of African American first graders attended schools that were between 90 percent and 100 percent African American. Nearly 50 percent of African American twelfth graders attended schools in which half or more of the students were African American. Of all groups, white children were the most segregated. Eighty percent of the white students in both the first and the twelfth grades attended schools that were between 90 percent and

100 percent white. According to this definition, a vast majority of American students—whites as well as African Americans—were being denied equality of educational opportunity.

That *The Coleman Report* documented the extent to which white students had successfully avoided desegregated schools is, in retrospect, not surprising, for *The Coleman Report* was based on information gathered in an era when the "Briggs dictum" prevailed. What was surprising was the failure of the investigators to find meaningful and significant differences between the schools to which African American students were assigned and the schools to which white students were assigned. That the survey was ordered and Coleman's remarks as it was getting underway suggest that there remained a prevailing belief that the quality of African American schools, as measured by the support or resources they received, differed markedly from that of white schools. It was also expected that the study would "establish that Southern states systematically discriminated against African Americans in the provision of school facilities," but "the tabulated data do not support the presumption of gross discrimination in the provision of school facilities in the South" (quoted in Mosteller & Moynihan, 1972, p. 10). The pattern of gross discrimination in the provision of resources for educational facilities and materials so evident in the South in the 1930s that Embree had documented, that Myrdal had reported in 1944, and that were testified to in the 1945 Senate hearings was not as great as it once was.

Differences between minority schools and majority schools were not as great as they once were but there were some differences. The researchers did find that: "There are fewer physics laboratories, there are fewer books per student in libraries, texts are less often in sufficient supply, schools are less often accredited, students who fail a subject are less likely to repeat a grade, they are less often schools with intensive testing, academically related extracurricular activities are less, the curriculum less often is built around an academic program" (Coleman, 1966, pp. 121–122). Such differences, however, were neither as "striking" nor as "significant" as had been expected. The researchers concluded that: "these differences in facilities and programs must not be overemphasized," for in many instances they were "not large." Moreover, they determined that "regional differences between schools are usually considerably greater than minority-majority differences" (p. 22).

Achievement Differences. The achievement differences among the groups the researchers identified and studied could not be explained by the differences in the schools the students attended. As Coleman (1966) noted, "it appears that variations in the facilities and curriculum of the schools account for relatively little variation in pupil achievement insofar as this is measured by standard tests" (p. 22). It seemed clear that: "Whatever may be the combination of nonschool factors—poverty, community attitudes, low educational level of parents—which put minority students at a disadvantage in verbal and nonverbal skills when they enter the first grade, the fact is the schools have not overcome it." The difference in achievement between minority students and majority students was significant. The difference in the academic achievement between African Americans and whites was found to be "progressively greater for the minority pupils at progressively higher grade levels" (p. 21). At age six, the "grade level gap" in achievement was 1.6 years. By the time students entered high school (grade nine) it was 2.4 years. At the end of school (grade twelve) it was up to 3.3 years. Minority students were at a disadvantage when they entered school. That disadvantage was even greater when they left school.

As late as 2008, educators were not able to claim that the achievement gap had been closed. Michael A. Rebell, an advocate of educational adequacy, observed that when "poor students of all races" enter the fifth grade, they "are two years behind their wealthier, predominantly white peers in reading and math." By the eighth grade, the gap is three years. By the twelfth grade, "the gap is a full four years" (Rebell, 2008, p. 433). There is some evidence that suggests that the achievement gap between high-achieving white students and high-achieving African American students persists and is growing (Viadero, 2008, pp. 1, 13).

Subsequent to *The Coleman Report* educators and educational researchers attended to how school practices and instruments for the measurement of school achievement affected populations that had previously been neglected and populations that were not achieving at a level equal to that of the majority population. Most important, a new measure for determining equality of educational opportunity was established. It was no longer sufficient to demonstrate that those who had been denied access to equal schools now had access to equal schools. It was no longer sufficient to demonstrate that students did not attend segregated schools. Academic achievement, as measured by standardized instruments, was becoming the accepted measure of equality of educational opportunity. By the beginning of the twenty-first century academic achievement became an important, if not the most important, measure of equality of educational opportunity. At the beginning of the twenty-first century when No Child Left Behind was enacted into law, educators were assigned the task of breaking the long established relationship between social-economic status and academic achievement as indicated by one's performance on standardized tests. The achievement gap became the accepted measure of inequality of educational opportunity, the greater the gap the greater the inequality.

Equality of educational opportunity continues to be an important topic on the education researchers' agenda as well as an important topic on the national agenda. Determining whether there exists equality of educational opportunity in public schools has turned out to not be a simple undertaking, for, as Coleman (1968) observed, there has been a "lack of stability in the concept" (p. 7).

Competition, Choice, and Alternatives

At a National Conference on Equal Educational Opportunity sponsored by the United States Commission on Civil Rights held in November 1967, four months after the appearance of *The Coleman Report,* Kenneth Clark whose research was cited in the *Brown* decision expressed his frustration with the failure of the nation to move toward extending equality of educational opportunity to all students. While some were trying to develop alternative modes of schooling within the existing school system and others were arguing that alternatives could only be developed outside the constraints imposed by existing public school systems, Clark offered a plan for alternative public school systems. It was a plan that essentially offered a new definition of public education. It was a definition that focused on neither who controlled public education nor how it was financed but on who benefitted from public education. His plan called for and relied on the principle of competition.

More than a decade after the Supreme Court declared that deliberately racially segregated schools were unconstitutional, Clark observed that there was still massive resistance to school desegregation in the North as well as in the South. He objected to the continuation of a "bi-racial system wherein approximately 90 per cent of American children are required to attend segregated schools" (Clark, 1968, p. 100). One system existed for poor or underprivileged children and another for privileged middle class children. Schools for the poor and schools for racial minorities were not as efficient as those provided for middle class children. According to Clark:

> This lower efficiency is expressed in terms of the fact that the schools attended by Negro and poor children have less adequate educational facilities than those attended by more privileged children. Teachers tend to resist assignments in Negro and other underprivileged schools and generally function less adequately in these schools. Their morale is generally lower; they are not adequately supervised; they tend to see their students as less capable of learning. (p. 101)

Inefficient schools were characterized by "cumulative academic retardation" (what is now known as the achievement gap), and "dropouts" who were not prepared for "a constructive role in society." Inefficient schools produced "a pattern of rejection and despair and hopelessness resulting in massive human wastage" (Clark, 1968, p. 101).

The cost of the schools' inefficiency for a society that would surely need fewer unskilled workers and more highly educated workers or more knowledgeable human capital was sure to be high. The public was paying to have the job of education done badly and would have to pay to have it done again because the poorly educated would have to be reeducated. Failure to provide equality of educational opportunity contributed "to the cycle of pathology—poor education, menial jobs or unemployment, family instability, group and personal powerlessness" (Clark, 1968, p. 102).

The forces in the way of allowing the nation's schools to fulfill their historic function of promoting social mobility were strong and came from both the white and the African-American sectors of the public. Besides the "more flagrant sources of opposition to any effective desegregation of American Public Schools," such as "the White Citizens' Councils in the South, parents, and taxpayers' groups in the North, and the control of boards of education by whites who identify either overtly or covertly with the more vehement opposition to change," there had developed, Clark maintained, "another formidable and insidious barrier in the way of the movement towards effective, desegregated public schools... in the form of the black power movement." Some African Americans were so frustrated that they "asserted that there should be separate school districts organized to control the schools in all-Negro residential areas; that there should be Negro Boards of Education, Negro superintendents of schools, Negro faculty, and Negro curricula and materials" (Clark, 1968, p. 103). While those demands were, according to Clark, an indication "that the quality of education in *de facto* segregated Negro schools in the North and the Negro schools in the South has steadily deteriorated under the present system of white control," such demands were unacceptable to Clark.

Clark suggested that rigorous attempts to improve the quality of education for underprivileged children might help the desegregation of schools, but he was not confident that improvements could be effected even though the social, human, and financial costs of inefficient schools were high. The obvious need for change would not necessarily produce change, because the public schools were tied to tradition. "They seem to represent," he claimed, "the most rigid forms of bureaucracies which, paradoxically, are most resilient in their ability and use of devices to resist rational demands for change." Public schools were able to resist change so easily because they were "protected monopolies" that had only token competition from private and parochial schools. In the absence of effective competition, the public schools had little reason to improve. "Alternatives—realistic, aggressive, and viable competitors—to the present public school systems" were, he insisted, necessary (Clark, 1968, pp. 110- 111).

Clark's Alternatives. The alternatives Clark described as "possible, realistic, and practical" included regional state schools that would be supported by states and would admit students from either side of the urban-suburban boundary; federal regional schools that would be supported from federal funds and would accept residential students; college- and university-related schools that would be supported by institutions of higher education "as part of their laboratories in education" and would admit students who were not the children of their faculty or their students; industrial demonstration schools that would be by financed by the private commercial sector but would be comprehensive schools rather than vocational schools; schools sponsored by labor unions for the children of their members as well as others; and Army schools that would be able to expand upon the Defense Department's efforts at reeducating "the casualties of our present public schools" (Clark, 1968, pp. 112–113).

Clark's proposals were founded on an affirmation of traditional American values. His claim was that competition worked in the private sector and it would work in public education. He was not abandoning his commitment to public education but he was offering a revised definition of public education. His concept of "public" was based on who benefitted from schooling regardless of the source of funding. His claim was that:

> ...public education need not be identified with the present system of organization of public schools. Public education can be more broadly and pragmatically defined in terms of that form of organization and functioning of an educational system which is in the public interest. (Clark, 1968, p. 111)

Clark was not calling for unregulated nineteenth-century *lassiez-faire* competition. He wanted the regulated competition of the modern liberal corporate state. Alternative public schools were to be regulated because the public had an interest in how well they functioned. While the alternative schools Clark proposed were to be "operated on a quasi-private level," they were to be subject to "quality control and professional accountability maintained and determined by Federal and State educational standards and supervision" (Clark, 1968, p. 113).

Clark believed that improving schools would improve society. Schools had served as "effective mobility vehicles for white American immigrants" and, if properly reformed, could do the same for the "influx of Negro and Puerto Rican youngsters into urban public schools." Inefficient schools constituted "clear threats to the viability of our cities and national stability" (Clark, 1968, p. 109). Efficient alternative systems of public education would, he maintained, free African American children from "lives of despair and hopelessness," save white children from "cynicism, moral emptiness, and social ineptness," and save "our civilization through saving our cities" (p. 113).

Clark's proposal for alternative public school systems reflected what proved to be the desire of many either to find alternatives to then existing public schools or to find a way to introduce effective reforms into the educational system that carried over into the twenty-first century. In the 1970s, some school systems established alternatives within their systems, and some alternatives received widespread attention. Some of the attention they received may have been due to their novelty, but not to the number of students they served. In 1973 Donald W. Robinson observed that: "Like all novelties, the alternative schools may have been given publicity out of all proportion to their numbers" (Robinson, 1973, p. 433). For example, one highly publicized alternative school—Philadelphia's Parkway School—was only capable of enrolling about 5 percent of the city's students.

Other Alternatives. Vernon H. Smith, a founder of the National Consortium on Options in Public Education and co-director of the Educational Alternatives Project at Indiana University, explained that the attention the media paid to a few alternatives, especially those in Chicago, Philadelphia, and Berkeley, contributed to the impression that alternatives were "bizarre experiments." He insisted, however, that alternative schools were established "to meet specific needs within their local communities." He agreed with Mario Fantini who claimed that alternative schools constituted "the only major movement in American education today" because alternatives were being developed not as an attempt by professional educators to comply with the requirements of a "national interest" but to realize the desires of people at the local level. Fantini[1] claimed that: "alternatives represent the first evolutionary thrust in public education at the grass-roots level" (Smith, 1973, p. 434). People at the grass-roots level were not then calling for more and better mathematics, science, and foreign language.

Smith reported that by the early 1970s eight different types of alternative schools had already been established in several communities. Some alternatives were merely attempts to comply with court orders to desegregate schools. "Open schools" individualized learning activities for students and organized learning activities "around interest centers within the classroom or building." "Schools without walls" were just that. Their students were directed, or allowed, to take advantage of "learning activities throughout the community" so they could learn about their world firsthand. A "magnet school," a "learning center," or "educational park" was designed to attract students from all parts of a community by concentrating resources and opportunities in one central location. Some magnet schools were established to encourage voluntary desegregation. "Multicultural schools," "bilingual schools," and "ethnic schools" focused on the diversity of cultures that existed in the nation's cities and emphasized "ethnic and racial awareness." "Street academies," "dropout centers," and "pregnancy-maternity centers" conducted programs for students whose needs could not easily be satisfied in conventional schools. A "school-within-a-school," could be any kind of alternative "with a voluntary population that is representative in racial, ethnic, and socioeconomic class makeup of the total population of the community." Still another type of alternative was the "free school," that, according to Smith (1973), was a term "usually applied to non-public alternatives," even though there were a few within public school systems (pp. 434–435). "Free" usually meant that teachers and students were free to do more of whatever they wanted to do. However, "free" did not necessarily mean an unstructured or informal classroom organized according to the current interests of students and teachers. "Free" did not mean that no tuition was charged.

Free Schools. Allen Graubard pointed out that at least four different types of free schools existed and that the differences among them were significant. A free school was not typically founded for a cross section of the population but for a particular portion of the population. The "classical" free school usually enrolled students of all ages and was modeled after A. S. Neil's Summerhill. The constituents of the "classical" free school, usually a boarding school, were typically from the white middle class. In those schools development of a student's personality was believed to be more important than academic achievement. Accordingly, the school's program was designed to "emphasize the emotional and expressive aspects of the personality rather than the formal academic curriculum or job preparation" (Graubard, 1972, p. 365).

The "parent–teacher cooperative elementary school" was usually a white middle class school. According to Graubard, such a school was usually founded by parents from the white middle class who were young, white, and liberal and who saw in the works of John Holt or Joseph Featherstone an alternative to the "regimentation of the normal public schools." In such schools, the "tuition is paid on a sliding scale and usually some minority students are admitted free or almost free." The cooperative schools had little appeal to poor minority parents who were typically most interested in their children's academic preparation and achievement. Cooperative schools were "not intended to confront the problems of ghetto families and their children." They were also different from "the relatively new, very progressive elementary schools." The progressive schools were "well-organized, well-equipped, fairly expensive, and rather professional about staffing, while the cooperatives had "looser organizations," less equipment, and less concern about professional staff (Graubard, 1972, p. 365).

The characteristics of the "free high school" varied according to the social class of its clientele. Some were "oriented toward the white middle class and hip youth cultures." Students who attended free high schools, and especially those who provided their "initial impetus," wanted "to be involved honestly in the planning and governance of their own school." Some projected "a politically radical perspective in their rhetoric, curriculum, and other activities" (Graubard, 1972, p. 366). They focused on then current political issues: the war in southeast Asia, the draft, the women's liberation movement, and the rights and problems of youth. They also participated in the civil rights movement and actively opposed the war in Viet Nam. The students in free high schools were "slated for college and high career achievement." "For them," Graubard observed, "the free high school is a way to get off, for a while at least, the beaten path to college and beyond" (p. 367).

The "permissiveness of the free school was often congenial to progressive middle-class parents," but the free school had "much less appeal to working-class parents who suspect that such experimental schools will not serve the needs of their children." Those parents persisted "in the hope that the American dream of working hard, getting skills and credentials, and making it in the world will somehow come true for their children" (Graubard, 1972, p. 366). Working-class parents who wanted free schools for their children were less in favor of providing opportunities for their children to be politically expressive than in having their children learn how to do well in school. Among the working-class, free high schools were the street academies—Harlem Prep was probably the most widely known—"where the pedagogy with its emphasis on skills is more conventional, and the strong commitment to getting the young people into college differs from the mood of the dominant free high school culture." These schools did, however, have an explicit political purpose in that they did "directly confront the tracking function of the public schools which 'prepare' these students for the lower rungs of the social and job hierarchy" (p. 367). Some of these schools did focus on what it meant to be a member of the working class in America but they also focused their attention on remedial work and vocational preparation.

Just as there were free high schools for the middle class and free high schools for the working class so were there free elementary schools for the same two classes, with differences similar to those between the two kinds of free high schools. "Community elementary schools" were founded by low-income parents who were "wary of romantic 'freedom and spontaneity' rhetoric," and who frequently favored "the more traditional classroom approaches, including strict discipline" (Graubard, 1972, pp. 367–368). Such schools were sometimes characterized by "pedagogical innovation" and a "libertarian atmosphere," but they were primarily interested in community control of schools. They did not oppose change, but they did oppose imposition of change because they had grown impatient and dissatisfied with the "system" that had been imposing changes and "failing their children for years." Such schools were closer to conventional schools in their practices than "cooperative elementary schools," but they did cast off some traditional school conventions. Graubard reported that "most of these schools had an aversion to fostering individual competition by means of grades." They preferred to give "each child a sense of his or her own worth and capacities" (Graubard, 1972, p. 368).

Advocates of free schools and alternative schools admitted that departures from conventional schooling were probably not suitable for all children. Graubard clearly indicated that the potential effect of free schools was indeed limited and acknowledged that "they have only been able to work with a very small number" (Graubard, 1972, p. 371). Vernon Smith recognized that "the few hundred alternative public schools in operation . . . have not yet had any effects on the mainstream of public education" but he believed that they did have "significant social and educational potential." He did not argue, as did Kenneth Clark, that public education needed competition. He was, however, not claiming that all schools had to be fashioned after the same model. He pointed out that the notion of choice was "consistent with a democratic philosophy, a pluralistic society, and a free market economy." His claim that "since the alternative school is an option within a community, it does not require consensus to justify its existence" was an admission that community consensus about public school programs was either not possible or not important. His claim that "alternatives can be developed to be responsive to the needs of minorities within the community" could mean that they served as a way to allow social and economic, if not racial and ethnic, segregation of schools to persist (Smith, 1973, p. 437). Smith indicated that alternatives could be an option to "forced busing" and further suggested that: "forced busing may become unnecessary in some communities as more students and their parents are able to choose from among voluntary integration models" (Smith, 1973, p. 436).

Graubard was not very sanguine about the future of the free school movement. His view was that "contrary to the predictions of some free education activists, this development will not mushroom into thousands of schools with hundreds of thousands of students." Besides the difficulties of maintaining them on a day-to-day basis, finding funds to support them, and that most Americans were content with the idea of the traditional public school, there was the possibility that "free-type schools supported by the system could be used to siphon off 'malcontents,' 'troublemakers,' and activists—between students and parents—and thus ease the spreading troubles in the public schools" (Graubard, 1972, p. 372).

Accountability

The accountability movement soon drew attention away from alternative schools and other educational innovations. Even when Vernon Smith was touting the significance and the importance of alternatives in education, he acknowledged that: "accountability is the word in public education today." He cited James Moffit, who had recently claimed that: "if we are serious about accountability, we would work it up from the people, not down to them, by replacing the present monopolistic, captive-clientele system of compulsory education with a free-choice, open-market competition of learning facilities" (Graubard, 1972, p. 372). According to Smith, accountability, responsiveness, and evaluation were all packed into the notion of alternatives. The alternatives for which a community opted would tell educators how well they were responding to the public's interests. He wanted alternatives to be offered on the educational marketplace so consumers could select what they wanted. However, the accountability movement did not allow that. Rather than expanding the range of options for parents, students, and educators, the accountability movement worked to restrict choice. School officials were not inclined to explore alternative approaches to schooling, for they were increasingly concerned with how well students performed on standardized tests. As Vito Perrone and Warren Strandbery reported:

> In our efforts at creating open classrooms we are increasingly confronted by school officials who say: "All that you advocate is fine but we have to be accountable." What they mean is that children must be at "grade-level" on various standardized achievement tests and exhibit some predetermined level of growth during the school year. Can an open classroom with an integrated

> curriculum be "risked" when school officials have such concerns? Administrators do not like to discuss issues such as whether children can be trusted to initiate more of their learning, or the community becoming a major learning environment. Instead, they question whether setting such directions will cause children to produce appropriate scores on a first grade standardized reading test or a third grade achievement test in social studies, mathematics, or science. (Perrone & Strandbery, 1972, pp. 347–348)

Those who endorse accountability claim that the school, as a public institution, is responsible to the public that pays for it and that the school has an obligation to show that it is conducting its mission responsibly, efficiently, and effectively by showing how well students perform on tests that allow comparisons to local, state, national, and even international norms. While few are inclined to argue that public schools should not be accountable, many object to how the measurement of the schools' effectiveness should be determined. Many also objected to the instruments—standardized tests—used to make and record the measurements. Attempts to make such measurements, some claim, interfere with the ends of education and the processes schools typically employ to achieve those ends. Attempts to measure school effectiveness are sometimes believed to have disruptive effects on schooling.

Accountability came with an ethos to which many educators objected. The authors of one critique maintained:

> The accountability movement is generating an ethos among educators that must not go unchallenged. This ethos—whose governing principles are based on a technological-economic world view—is distinguished by its frenzied insistence on the large-scale transportation of attitudes and practices from the world of business, engineering, and science to the world of education. One result of this slavish dependence on the beliefs and procedures of other fields has been to reduce the total educational endeavor to a tired litany of achievement, performance, and production characterized by the blank torpor of systems analysis, technological engineering, quality control, and replicability. (Nash & Agne, 1972, p. 357)

For such critics, there was clearly a "myopic fixation on the means of accountability, to the systematic exclusion of any serious concern with ends" (Nash & Agne, 1972, p. 360).

The emergence of the accountability movement can be attributed to the public's dissatisfaction with public education and, to some extent, the public's concern with the attention that was being given to the needs of disadvantaged and minority children. Some accepted the calls for accountability because they believed the schools were failing to educate their children.

The failures of their children and their subsequent difficulties and disappointments on the job market supported their belief in the schools' inability to fulfill their responsibilities effectively and fairly. In some instances, groups demanded community control of the schools to ensure a measure of accountability. In light of such demands, the results of standardized tests often seemed a better way to satisfy those demands or to answer critics' charges than testimony (no matter how sincere, detailed, or impassioned) about what schools and teachers did on behalf of their students.

Some who called for strict accountability measures were doubtless disturbed by and unsympathetic toward the schools' effort to make public education more joyful or the schools' attempts to develop effective programs for disadvantaged and minority children. For those who were concerned with ever-increasing tax rates for ever larger school budgets to pay for programs for those whom they believed did not pay taxes, accountability was an attractive solution. Accountability meant that public schools would have to show results and ask for fewer resources. It meant cutting out frills and getting back to basics. The emphasis on returning to basics and accountability may have been motivated more by economic, social, and political interests than by educational concerns (Martin, Overholt, & Urban, 1976, p. 49).

Educators had to respond to the calls for accountability because the federal government not only supported the movement but also in some instances demanded accountability. One of accountability's chief enthusiastic promoters was Leon Lessinger, a former official from the United States Office of Education. He was called its "high priest," and his book, *Every Kid a Winner*, its "bible." Lessinger's claims were simple. All children, regardless of their racial, ethnic, or social background, were entitled to an education that would prepare them to be productive adults. The public had a right to know how schools spent money and what results were achieved with the money they spent.

Lessinger likened public education to a very complicated machine and educational experts to engineers. Educational engineers were to determine how the machine worked, what its difficulties and malfunctions were, and then prescribe in precise terms how the machine could be modified to effect specified results. Lessinger defined education in behavioral terms. Educational engineers were to assist in specifying educational outcomes in precise measurable terms, work out the technology for their realization, show what the cost of producing the outcomes would be, and assist in finding external auditors who were to determine whether the established outcomes had been met by the schools. The focus of the educational engineers was narrower than that of the conventional educator who often used factors external to schooling to explain students' failures. Accountability advocates claimed to look only at what occurred in the school's classroom and were thus charged with ignoring important social factors that influence student success or failure. To the extent that external social factors were used as an excuse or justification for failing to serve all students fairly and effectively, Lessinger's position had considerable merit. It was also either a denial or a rejection of what was reported in *The Coleman Report* or an adumbration of what No Child Left Behind would require.

As with any proposal that challenges the established educational organization and its practices, some critics pointed out that it was not actually new (Martin et al., 1976, ch 3). One feature of accountability—payment by results—had been tried in England in the nineteenth century. There the practice of allocating funds to schools according to how well students scored on the school inspectors' standard examinations resulted in the creation of a narrow curriculum. Teachers taught to the test and eliminated topics not likely to be on the inspectors' examinations. After enactment of No Child Left Behind, some claimed that teachers were being forced to teach to the tests students were required to pass.

The Technological Perspective. Accountability can be viewed as an aspect of what Ernest R. House identified as the technological perspective in educational innovation. Up to the mid 1960s, according to House, the strategy used for promoting change in education was "scholastic authority." Scholars from universities developed new materials and methods they believed appropriate and necessary and disseminated them through various publications and through workshops for teachers. It was then assumed that if given new information, teachers would use it. By the mid 1960s, that approach began to give way to a technological view of educational change that conceptualized the educational process "as separated into functions based on rational analysis and empirical research." The new approach required that all assumptions be made explicit, analyzed, and tested empirically. This approach was believed to have worked in other sectors of society, and so, it was believed it would also work in education. According to House (1981):

> There were important models for this rationalization of the innovation process. Both modern industry and modern agriculture were highly successful. Space technology was occupying the front pages of newspapers. Technologized processes seemed to be related to progress. Progress was achieved by introducing new techniques into an area, and the process of modernization itself could be systematized, organized, and replicated. (p. 21)

From the technological perspective, teaching "could be improved by the introduction of new techniques" (House, 1981, p. 21). Teachers were assumed to be completely fungible. The outcomes of schooling were to be improved by enhancing the skills and knowledge of the teachers by creating better materials and methods for their use. The model for introducing changes into schools was "R-D-D": *Research* was to be *developed* into useable forms and then *diffused* through all educational systems. It was assumed that what worked in one place would work equally well in another place if the teachers were properly trained. It was a model that held that individuals were psychobiological entities that develop in specified and predictable patterns and stages that are universal. Adoption of this perspective was vigorously supported. According to House, "more than twenty federal research and development laboratories and centers were established with this model in mind" (House, 1981, p. 22). He further reported that: "government funding has gone overwhelmingly into studies and projects conducted from the technological perspective" (p. 41). The federal government's expenditures to evaluate programs with procedures based on the technological perspective also increased significantly after the mid 1960s. Before 1964, "no more than a few hundred thousand dollars were spent annually on educational program evaluation." By 1970, the expenditure for program evaluation was $5million a year (Cohen & Garet, 1975, p. 18). By 1975 the federal government was spending about $100 million a year on research and development projects based on the technological perspective.

Management by Objectives. By 1973, Sidney P. Marland, Jr., the United States Commissioner of Education, acknowledged that accountability had been "a relatively fumbling, ad hoc process." He also claimed that there was reason to believe the future would be different and better. New dimensions of accountability promised "better organized and more precise methods of measurement." He reported that: "efforts are being made to establish objectives in more systematic ways." "Management by objectives," was, he related, "an important key to the smooth operation of our contemporary educational institutions" (Marland, 1972, p. 339). He admitted that not all educational considerations and goals were easily stated in precise, measurable terms but was not willing to abandon the effort. Education was unlike product development in a research laboratory where even complex goals and processes were "relatively tangible and capable of definition." It was indeed difficult to tell how various events and experiences influenced students. As Marland related:

> But who is to say what happens in the heart and mind of a 10-year-old when he perceives for the first time the breach, let us say, of a democratic ideal?

> An unintended brush off by a teacher? The academic failure or triumph of a friend? How does it affect him and his view of life, of truth, his home, his school, his community? (p. 342)

Such considerations were indeed "vague" and "difficult to apply yardsticks to." Still, Marland maintained that if "we establish goals such as 'the socialization of the child'," then it was necessary "to verbalize these goals in measurable terms." An alternative he did not specify but one adopted by some in response to the demand that all objectives be stated in behavioral terms was simply to abandon those educational goals and purposes that could not be easily and simply stated and easily measured.

For Marland, accountability raised many "pertinent questions." They included:

> How productively are our teachers being used, and how effectively is their time and wisdom being applied to the needs of the learner? What technology is available to multiply greatly the teachers' talent? What is the full scope of the university professor's mission? (Marland, 1972, p. 344)

In the systems approach employed by the advocates of accountability, Marland found a "beauty" that promised to reveal "new methods, new techniques, new materials, new ways to motivate young people, and indeed, new ways to define objectives" (Marland, 1972, p. 342).

Note

1. Fantini's statement was from a speech he delivered at a regional conference on options in public education at Grand Rapids, Michigan, November 1, 1972.

7

From A Nation at Risk *to No Child Left Behind*

Introduction

In the 1980s, the nation's need for knowledgeable human capital and the need to extend equality of educational opportunity to all the nation's children and youth—the two issues that had dominated education discourse at the national level since the end of World War II—were no longer being seen as separate issues but as issues that were clearly and inextricably related to each other. In the 1980s, it was clearly recognized that the nation could not compete in the Global Economy unless it had the requisite supply of knowledgeable human capital. By the end of the twentieth century it was clear that the nation would not have that supply unless it found a way to close the achievement gap that Coleman had identified in the mid-1960s. By the beginning of the twenty-first century, it was becoming increasing clear that the nation was and would continue to experience significant demographic changes and that the nation's schools were faced with finding ways to serve successfully populations that historically had not been served successfully.

Equality of Educational Opportunity and Knowledgeable Human Capital, pages 127–152

No Child Left Behind was designed to close the achievement gap or what *The Coleman Report* described as the "grade-level gap." *The Coleman Report* basically argued that schools were not totally responsible for the failure of some students, especially disadvantaged students, to achieve and that there was a strong and consistent relationship between students' academic achievement and the social conditions where they were nurtured and educated. However, No Child Left Behind was based on the belief that the school and its teachers were totally responsible for students' academic achievement.

The Reports of the 1980s

The emphasis on extending equality of educational opportunity in the mid 1960s and early 1970s to those who had been earlier denied that opportunity, took some attention away from the nation's need for knowledgeable human capital and the accompanying concern with how few students were successfully studying mathematics, science, and foreign language. It did not, however, remove those concerns from the national education agenda. A report ordered by President James E. Carter and prepared by the National Science Foundation and the Office of Education claimed that the rigor of mathematics and science programs in the nation's public schools was less than those in the schools in the Soviet Union, Japan, and Germany. According to the report, "the number of young people who graduate from high school and college with only the most rudimentary notions of science, mathematics and technology portend trouble in the decades ahead." Unless "the current trend toward virtual scientific and technological illiteracy" is reversed, the report warned, many will be making important decisions in the future "on the basis of ignorance and misunderstanding" (National Science Foundation and Department of Education, 1980, p. 3).

By the early 1980s, the media were reporting that public education had deteriorated so badly that the nation was faced with a major education crisis. That for nearly two decades educators had been directed to extend equality of educational opportunity to those who had been earlier excluded or ill-served by public education was somehow then overlooked. That educational opportunities, especially if measured by access, had indeed been extended to more students than ever before was also overlooked. As Diane Ravitch (1981) reported:

> At mid-century, about 50 percent graduated from high school; the figure today is 85 percent. From 1968 to 1978, black enrollments grew from 6.4 percent to more than 10 percent of all college students, and the proportion of

> females increased from 39 percent to 48 percent. For the first time in our history, access to higher education is universal.... One-third of post-secondary institutions are "open door," accepting all applicants regardless of their academic credentials; more than half are "selective," accepting only those who meet their qualifications, but nonetheless accepting most or all of those who apply for admission; and just eight percent are "competitive," accepting only a portion of qualified applicants. (p. 24)

As reported in the *New York Times* in 1983, significant progress had been made in teaching basic skills to minority students, students from low-income families, and "those who were weakest academically" (Fiske, 1983). As an official from the National Institute of Education observed, "We have made a big turnaround in teaching the most basic skills to the lowest quartile of kids... but in raising the floor we have at best kept the ceiling constant" (quoted in Fiske, 1983). By the early 1980s, there was concern that the basic skills, that over two-thirds of the states had specified as minimum competencies in the 1970s, consisted only of "low order skills, such as the literal comprehension of a reading passage" and did not include "the abstract reasoning and problem-solving skills that are expected to become increasingly important in the emerging technological society" (Fiske, 1983). The emphasis on "basic skills" and "minimum competencies" was giving way to a renewed interest in excellence and academic achievement. Excellence and academic achievement were securing more attention and currency than resources, access, or integration. Achievement was becoming the preferred measure of equality of educational opportunity.

SAT Scores. Falling scores on the Scholastic Aptitude Test (SAT) alarmed some education critics. Between 1963 and 1980, the median verbal score on the SAT fell from a high of 478 to 424, and the median score on the mathematical portion of the SAT fell from 502 to 466. The immediate explanation for the declining SAT scores, once they were observed, was that more female, more minority students, and more students from low-income families were sitting for the test and not doing as well as those who had traditionally sat for the test. That explanation did not hold up. Analysis of the composition of those who had been sitting for the test revealed that since 1970 the composition of those who sat for the test did not change significantly. However, the scores fell more dramatically in the 1970s than they did in the 1960s. In fact, when the decline appeared to end in 1982, the College Board explained that the improved average scores could be attributed to the improved scores made by minority students. By 1984, the College Board was able to report that the nine-point increase in test scores (five points on the verbal portion and four points on the mathematical portion) was the largest single year gain since 1963. While the decrease in the number of African American students sitting for the test was "disturbing," it was reported that that decrease did not affect the average test scores (Currence, 1984, p. 4).

As significant to education critics as the decline in average SAT scores was the decline in the percent of students who scored between 600 and 800 on the verbal part of the SAT. Between 1972 and 1981, the percent of students scoring between 600 and 800 on the verbal part fell from 11.4 to 7, and the decline on the mathematical part was from 17.8 to 14.5 percent. In 1982, there were increases in high scores, but they did not match the high scores of the early 1970s. The percent of those who scored between 600 and 800 on the mathematical portion of the test increased from 14.5 to 15.2 percent, but the increase on the verbal portion was a modest 0.1 percent (Fiske, 1983).

Claims that there was something peculiar about the SAT also failed to withstand examination. Annegret Harnischfeger and David E. Wiley analyzed student performances on other tests (the ACT, the Iowa Test of Basic Skills, and the Minnesota Scholastic Aptitude Test) and found declines similar to those on the SAT (Ravitch, 1981, p. 25). Their study revealed that students who enrolled in the traditional college preparatory curriculum—the kind of curriculum earlier recommended by the Committee of Ten—did well on the tests. Those who avoided the traditional curriculum did less well. Students did not do well on tests that tested what they had not studied. Few noted that students had little reason to enroll in courses that colleges no longer required for admission.

Many explanations were offered for the poor test scores: Vietnam, Watergate, "the rights revolutions," drugs, broken homes, the increased number of working mothers, television, computer games, busing, and government programs designed to remedy longstanding social and economic discrimination. The 1960s, the decade during which SAT scores began to decline, was a decade of significant expansion of public secondary education. The number of high school teachers nearly doubled during that decade (from 575,000 to 1 million). Paul Copperman claimed that the expansion of secondary education set the stage "for an academic tragedy of historic proportions as the nation's high school faculty, about half of whom were young and immature, prepare to meet the largest generation of high school students in American history" (quoted in "Help! Teacher Can't Teach," 1980, p. 58).

A Nation at Risk. As evidenced by a number of commissions and reports in the 1980s, there was still another campaign to reform the nation's schools, to restore them to what some believed they had been but no longer were. The appearance of many reports, especially *A Nation at Risk*, is said to have "spurred the greatest national debate on education since the launching of *Sputnik* in 1957" (Stedman & Smith, 1983, p. 85). It turned out to be a government report on education in the United States that "catapulted education near to the top of the national political agenda, helping to pave the way for a further extension of the federal role in the nation's school districts" (Davies, 2007, p. 5).

"The widespread public perception that something is seriously remiss in our educational system" (National Commission, 1983, p. 1) was the reason President Ronald Reagan's Secretary of Education Terrel Bell gave for appointing the National Commission on Excellence in Education. The Commission agreed with Bell that there was reason for concern and agreed with what had been continually claimed since the end of World War II—the welfare of the nation depended on the quality of its public schools. It reported that the world had become "one global village" populated by "determined, well educated, and strongly motivated competitors." In the global village, "knowledge, learning, information, and skilled intelligence" were "the new raw materials of international commerce" and were "spreading throughout the world as vigorously as miracle drugs, synthetic fertilizers, and blue jeans did earlier" (pp. 6–7) The Commission warned the nation that: "The educational foundations of our society are presently being eroded by a rising tide of mediocrity that threatens our very future as a nation and a people." The nation had "squandered the gains in student achievement made in the wake of the Sputnik challenge" (p. 5).

The Commission on Excellence (1983) received ample testimony to allow it to claim that earlier gains had been lost and that nation was at risk at a time "when the demand for highly skilled workers in new fields is accelerating rapidly" (p. 10). Compared to international students, American students' achievement was not competitive. American students failed to rank first or second on nineteen academic achievement tests and ranked last seven times. Between 1963 and 1980 student scores on the verbal portion of the Scholastic Aptitude Test declined more than fifty points. The decline on the mathematics portion was more than forty points. Scores in English and physics were also declining. Whether judged by the proportion of students or the absolute number of students, the decline of those earning a superior score—650 or higher—"dramatically declined." College students' achievement was not as high as it was earlier. Assessments of high-school-age students in science in 1969, 1973, and 1977 showed declines. Approximately 13 percent of that same cohort was "functionally illiterate and as many as 40 percent of minority youth were functionally illiterate. Among students classified as gifted, there was a gap between their ability and their actual achievement. Schools were not producing the knowledgeable human capital the nation needed. "Business and military leaders complain that they are required to spend millions of dollars on costly remedial education and training programs in such basic skills as reading, writing, spelling, and computation" (pp. 8–9).

That the Reagan administration's federalism was designed to restore control of education to local and to state authorities was recognition that the federal government—an agency with the responsibility for expressing and protecting the national interest—had admitted an interest in education and had acted on that interest. The Commission maintained that: "The Federal Government has *the primary responsibility* to identify the national interest in education." It further suggested that the federal government had an obligation to "fund and support efforts to protect and promote that interest" (National Commission, 1983, p. 33, emphasis in original).

The Reagan administration ensured that education would be high on the national agenda not only by commissioning and publishing *A Nation at Risk* but also by distributing and promoting it. *A Nation at Risk* received a great deal of attention because the deliberate campaign to ensure that it would receive attention was successful. On April 26, 1983, two hundred invited representatives of American education, business, and government witnessed Secretary of Education Terrell Bell present President Ronald Reagan with a copy of *A Nation at Risk,* the report of the National Commission on Excellence in Education that Bell, not President Reagan, had appointed in 1981.

Five months after *A Nation at Risk* was presented to President Reagan, two of the Commission's staff reported that: "the tumultuous reception of the report by the press and the public has yet to subside" (Goldberg & Harvey, 1983, p. 14). It received coverage from print media—for example, *Time, Newsweek, U.S. News & World Report,* and several newspapers—and the electronic media—"The NcNeil-Lehrer Report," "Good Morning America," and "Nightline." Within five months after its presentation to President Reagan, 200,000 copies had been printed and several newspapers printed portions of it for their readers. It was soon followed by several other "national reports" on education.[1] By July 1983, according to the staff director of the National Commission on Excellence in Education, "nearly three million copies of... *A Nation at Risk,* had been distributed by the Government Printing Office or indirectly through reprints in professional publications and newspapers" (Clark, Astuto, & Rooney, 1983, p. 188).

Other National Reports. By 1984, it was estimated that were nearly thirty national reports that held that "excellence must be found and returned to the schools" and that the states had appointed nearly three hundred task forces and "sent them forth in search of excellence" (Cross, 1984, p. 168). Two years after publication of *A Nation at Risk* Charles Strickland (1985) observed:

> The recent avalanche of reports on education in these United States will leave anyone aged more than fifty with a sense of *deja vu*. After nearly thirty years the schools and their problems are moving once again to the center of the nation's consciousness. Once again we hear the litany about the mediocrity of the schools, followed by demands for excellence. Once again we hear a call for a tightening of standards and a toughening of discipline. Once again, the nation's welfare and security are invoked as the justification for educational reform. Once again, the focus of concern is on the neglect of those subjects which promise technological superiority. (p. 15)

The attention given to *A Nation at Risk* and the subsequent reports not only indicated to Americans that the public schools were once again facing a crisis but also indicated that, notwithstanding the rhetoric about local control and the Reagan administration's desire to return control and responsibility back to the states and local communities, public education was high on the national agenda. For the Reagan administration, education was "a national *concern* but a state and local *responsibility*." As such, education was "high on the national agenda but low in his [Reagan's] budgetary priorities" (Clark et al., 1983, p. 191; see also Levin, 1982, p. 456).

The vocabulary of war and national survival was employed in *A Nation at Risk* to incite Americans to action: "If an unfriendly foreign power had attempted to impose on America the mediocre performance that exists today, we might well have viewed it as an act of war" (National Commission, 1983, p. 3). The Task Force for Economic Growth agreed and advised that the nation was facing a "real emergency" and argued that improvement of public education was "crucial to our national survival" (pp. 2, 9). The Soviet threat was not invoked but fear of successful foreign competition in the economic arena was. The Commission on Excellence reminded Americans that "the Japanese make automobiles more efficiently than Americans," that "the South Koreans recently built the world's most efficient steel mill," and that "American machine tools, once the pride of the world, are being replaced by German products." The only way for the nation to retain its "slim competitive edge" was through an improved education system. "Learning," advised the Commission, was "the indispensable investment required for success in the 'information age' we are entering" (National Commission, 1983, pp. 6–7). As Harold Howe II, a former United States Commissioner of Education, observed, the prevailing thinking was that: "Better schools that produce better-educated workers are thought to be the way to outsell the Japanese and the Germans" (Howe, 1983, p. 188).

About a month after *A Nation at Risk* appeared, the Twentieth Century Fund, a private foundation devoted to the study of social, political, and economic issues, released a report it had commissioned a twelve-member panel of scholars and educators to assemble. While the National Commission on Excellence in Education reported that: "the educational foundations of our society are presently being eroded by a rising tide of mediocrity that threatens our future as a nation and a people" (National Commission, 1983, p. 5), the Fund's panel advised that "the nation's public schools are in trouble." According to the panel, "by almost every measure—the commitment and competency of teachers, student test scores, truancy and dropout rates, crimes of violence—the performance of our schools falls far short of expectations"[2] A report conducted by the National Task Force on Education for Economic Growth, sponsored by the Educational Commission of the States, echoed the concerns expressed in *A Nation at Risk*. The Task Force observed that the nation had asked and therefore had received "too little of our schools over the past two decades." Consequently, schools were "not doing an adequate job of education for today's requirements in the workplace, much less tomorrow's" (Green, 1983, p. 1).

Even before the publication of *A Nation at Risk*, many politicians expressed their desire for "educational eminence" and called for educational reform. A variety of commissions and study groups recommended that junior high school and high school students enroll in fewer electives and concentrate on the study of mathematics, science, English, and foreign languages. In California, then Governor Jerry Brown personally delivered a resolution to the state board of education. He asked that all high school students be required to complete three years of mathematics, two years of science, and one-half year of computer science as well as courses in arts and literature. He had earlier presented an even more rigorous proposal to the University of California regents. He requested the regents to set new admission requirements that would require a fourth year of mathematics for all students who applied for admission to the University of California. After the appearance of *A Nation at Risk*, the Superintendent for Public Instruction for the State of California, William Honig, proclaimed that: "more children than we ever expected *can* succeed in an intensive academic curriculum—not necessarily physics and calculus, but a strong common core of history, government, science and literature" (Honig, 1985, p. 675).

Ohio State University rescinded its practice of admitting any Ohio high school graduate and announced that it planned to admit only students who had completed a traditional college preparatory program (four years of English, a foreign language, and three years of social studies, science, and mathematics). Nebraska adopted a similar policy, effective in 1986. Florida also moved in a similar direction. The State College Board of Mississippi announced that beginning in 1986 all students would have to complete three years of science and three years of mathematics to qualify for admission to the state's colleges. In 1982, Iowa's Governor Robert Ray indicted that there was a need for more and better foreign language courses in Iowa's schools and colleges. Such an improvement would presumably help sell Iowa's agricultural products on foreign markets (Pipho, 1982, p. 5). According to the Education Commission for the States, by 1987, several states had increased high school graduation requirements. Mathematics requirements were increased in forty-two states. Science requirements were increased in thirty-six states. Foreign language requirements or electives were increased in five states (Boyer, 1991, p. 180).

While the National Commission on Excellence in Education was preparing *A Nation at Risk*, others were addressing the public's declining confidence in and support for public schools. Michael W. Kirst studied the declining support for the nation's secondary schools and concluded that the public's perception was that the schools "standards, rigor, and quality have slipped." The curriculum was neither what it once was nor what it should be. Three major reasons why the curriculum had been "debased" were:

1. an overattention to the legitimate needs of those in the bottom band of the achievement distribution, which has caused neglect of the college-bound and lowered the instructional center of gravity;
2. a preoccupation with process and technique, and with procedural accountability, finance, and governance, to the detriment of what we teach; and
3. a lack of emphasis on the usefulness and relevance of our common cultural heritage (Kirst, 1981).

To restore public confidence in public education educators needed to present students with "challenging academic material." The subtext was clear: The attention given to ensuring that those whose access to equal educational opportunity had been restricted or denied would be given what had been restricted or denied was achieved at the expense of academic achievement or excellence in education. The "gifted" students were once again being neglected. However, the National Commission on Excellence held that the talents of all children and youth had to be developed to their "fullest." The Commission maintained that: "The twin goals of equity and high-quality schooling have profound and practical meaning for our economy and society, and we cannot permit one to yield to the other either in principle or in practice" (National Commission, 1983, p. 13).

One year before the National Commission recommended that all high school students be required to complete "*Five New Basics*" (four years of English; three years of mathematics; three years of science; three years of social studies; and one-half year of computer science) (National Commission, 1983, p. 24), Gene I. Maeroff, an education writer for the *New York Times*, recommended that schools be freed from responsibility for solving social ills so they could focus on what they do best. It was, he claimed, necessary to distinguish between education and schooling and admit that all of education cannot be assigned to schools: "Let the schools be free to concentrate on the teaching of literacy in all its forms, a job that no other agency is pursuing or is as well equipped to address" (Maeroff, 1982, p. 12). Maeroff suggested that since public confidence in public schools had declined just when so many responsibilities had been assigned to them, they would be better off if they could free themselves of such responsibilities, for example, desegregation of society, sex education, and driver education. He did not want schools to accept responsibilities that belonged either to parents or to other social agencies.

Almost thirty years after Bestor called for a restoration of an earlier educational regime, the authors of *A Nation at Risk* called for students to return to study of the traditional school subjects. Just as Bestor had so the authors of *A Nation at Risk* presented statistics to document the decline they perceived. They warned that: "the public has no patience with undemanding and superfluous offerings" (National Commission, 1983, p. 17). High School curricula, they claimed, were "homogenized, diluted, and diffused to the point that they no longer have a central purpose." In the curricula smorgasbord, "the appetizers and deserts can easily be mistaken for the main course." The choices students made from the "cafeteria-style curriculum" were reported with statistics reminiscent of Bestor's. Between 1964 and 1979, enrollment in general programs of study as opposed to vocational or college preparatory programs increased from 12 percent to 42 percent, and at least a fourth of such programs were far from the traditional course of study. "Twenty-five percent of the credits earned by general track high school students are in physical and health education, work experience outside school, remedial English and mathematics, and personal service development courses, such as training for adulthood and marriage" (National Commission, 1983, p. 19). Intermediate algebra was offered in most high schools, but only 31 percent of students competed that course. While 60 percent of the students had the opportunity to enroll in calculus, only

6 percent of those who enrolled completed the course. Only 13 percent completed French I.

The publication of *A Nation at Risk* was followed by "at least 30 other national studies of education, 290 state commission and blue-ribbon task force reports, two network television documentaries, and widespread newspaper and magazine coverage of the problems of public schools" ("Renegotiating Society's Contract with the Public Schools," 1985, p. 2). In addition, after having been presented with *A Nation at Risk*, President Reagan focused attention on the need to reform public education. By June 1983, Gene I. Maeroff was able to report that: "Ronald Reagan is crisscrossing America charging that the schools have become 'just too soft and easy'." President Reagan "attended regional meetings sponsored by the Commission on Excellence; visited local schools in Kentucky, Tennessee, Kansas, and California; spoke to the American Federation of Teachers and the National Parent/Teacher Association; and hosted two meetings of major education associations at the White House" (Clark et al., 1983, p. 188). The president's efforts were effective. Educational reform, he reported, had become "a topic of political debate at the highest levels and teachers may no longer be able to escape the calls for reform" (Maeroff, 1983).

There is some suggestion that setting academic standards may affect positively students' academic performance. For example, for most of the 1990s, the state of Minnesota had no state standards for mathematics and science. After adopting standards in 1998, Minnesota students' scores were above national averages in four categories—fourth and eighth grade mathematics and science—measured by TIMSS (Trends in International Mathematics and Science Study). From 1995 when Minnesota first participated in TIMSS to 2007, its fourth grade mathematics scores increased by thirty-eight points, from 516 to 554 on a 1,000-point scale. Minnesota's scores in eighth grade mathematics, and fourth and eighth grade science were "all higher than the international TIMSS average" and with the exception of fourth grade science "statistically higher than the U.S. average in every major TIMSS category" (Cavanagh, 2009, p. 12).

Students from the United States did better on the mathematics and science tests than they did in 1995. However, students from Massachusetts and from Minnesota, states that took part in TIMSS separately achieved a level higher than the United States, and "Massachusetts did as well as some of their Asian peers" ("U.S. Betters Math Scores," 2008, p. 24). Massachusetts, a state that had been praised for setting "clear and demanding academic standards," was the only other U.S. State that participated in TIMSS in 1995 and 2007. Its scores in fourth and eighth grade mathematics and science were above both U.S. and international averages (Cavanagh, 2009, p. 12).

The emphasis on standards and excellence in the many reports that comprised the "excellence movement" prompted some to ask whether the movement was for the benefit of some, but not all, American students. An analysis of reports published by the National Commission on Secondary Education for Hispanics and the National Board of Inquiry into Schools conducted by Bernard Lefkowitz suggested that "the relative inattention to changes required for education of minority, low-income, female, and handicapped youngsters is a critical flaw in the current drive for educational excellence" ("Renegotiating Society's Contract," 1985, p. 2). Ernest L. Boyer, president of the Carnegie Foundation for the Advancement of Teaching asked: "Do we mean excellence for all or for the privileged few?" (p. 2).

The Carnegie Task Force

In January 1985, the Carnegie Corporation of New York established the Carnegie Forum on Education and the Economy. The Forum's purpose was to draw the nation's attention to the relationship between the nation's economic growth and "the skills and abilities of the people who contribute to that growth" and to formulate education policies for the economic challenges the nation was facing (The Carnegie Forum, 1986, p. iii). The Forum accepted the suggestion of its Advisory Council3 and appointed a Task Force chaired by Lewis M. Branscomb,[4] IBM's chief scientist, to examine teaching as a profession and to make appropriate recommendations.

The Carnegie Task Force, as Tumin and Bressler had and as the National Commission on Excellence did, rejected any suggestion that the nation had to choose to emphasize either quality or equity. The nature of the world economy in which the nation was competing gave the nation no choice but to opt for quality and equity. Because the nation's economy was clearly "technology-based," those who were poorly educated but "willing to work hard" could no longer find work. The cost of not providing a quality education to all the nation's children, including the one out of every four who were born into poverty, was a cost the nation could not long afford.

If the nation was to continue to maintain the standard of living it had attained and avoid "the growth of a permanent underclass," the majority of the students graduated by the nation's schools needed to be graduated "with achievement levels long thought possible for only the privileged few." The nation could only prosper if it sought new standards of excellence and strove "to make quality and equality of opportunity with each other" (Carnegie Forum, 1986, p. 21).

American businesses were already spending "billions of dollars a year retraining people who arrive at the workplace with inadequate education" (Carnegie Forum, 1986, p. 14). Employers were complaining that too many of their employees, even college graduates, were not able "to read complicated material, evaluate or make complex arguments, write well, or apply quantitative concepts and methods to unfamiliar problems." The recent gains students had made on standardized tests reflected gains in basic skills. Those gains were misleading and insufficient for they only showed progress on "earlier standards." Basic competence was no substitute for the "ability to reason and perform complex non-routine intellectual tasks" (pp. 15, 20).

As was to be expected, the Task Force recommended the restructuring of public schools, the teaching force, and the programs that educated and trained teachers. The Task Force was acutely away of the demographic changes occurring in the nation. African Americans, Hispanics, and Asians were fast becoming "rising proportion of the school population." In California, a majority of the students in the first three grades were minorities. In twenty-three of twenty-five of the largest city school systems, a majority of the students were minorities. At the same time, the proportion of teachers from minority groups fell far short of the proportion of minority students in the nation's schools. The need for minority teachers was great. To satisfy that need the Task Force urged leaders in colleges and universities to "strengthen existing programs, develop new ones, and find the funds necessary for both" (Carnegie Forum, 1986, p. 84).

While the Task Force clearly wanted teachers to improve their performance and to be more productive, it was not willing to hold teachers solely responsible for the educational deficiencies the nation was facing. Improvement required significant changes in a system that was "overwhelmingly bureaucratic." The Task Force maintained that it was "unreasonable to hold teachers accountable for results when many of the important decisions about how students' needs are to be met are made by others" (Carnegie Forum, 1986, p. 89).

By 1987, the nation's "economic misfortunes" and the realization that nations once seen as "economically and technologically inferior" were successfully competing and even surpassing the United States suggested to John F. Jennings, counsel for the U.S. House of Representatives' Committee on Education and Labor, that the economic challenges the nation faced were not unlike the challenge *Sputnik* presented thirty years earlier. According to Jennings (1987):

> The Sputnik of the 1980s is economic competition, and the United States is beginning to recognize that the educational attainment of its people is an intrinsic element of national economic well-being. Just as in 1957, a consensus is forming in favor of a federal response to this grave challenge. (p. 104)

Jennings' observation that there was a strong relationship between the nation's supply of knowledgeable human capital and its ability to be economically competitive proved to be an observation that President George H. W. Bush and then President William J. Clinton agreed with and acted upon.

Civics Achievement. While there was concern about how well students were performing in those subjects—mathematics, science, and foreign languages—most reformers emphasized, attention was directed toward other subjects. For example, at the end of the 1980s, the National Center for Educational Statistics contracted with Educational Testing Services (ETS) to summarize two surveys that the National Assessment of Educational Progress (NAEP) to assess the nations' students' achievement in civics. One was a "trend assessment" of students at ages thirteen and seventeen conducted during the 1975–76, 1981–2, and 1987–88 school years. The other was an assessment conducted in 1988 of students in the fourth-, eighth-, and twelfth-grades (National Assessment of Educational Progress, 1990, p. 6).

The summary ETS completed revealed that there were no significant or outstanding gains in civic achievement over the twelve-year period, that minority students achieved less well than white students, and that students from "advantaged urban areas" or rural areas performed better than those from "disadvantaged urban areas."

In 1988, seventeen-year-olds did not perform as well as did their counterparts in either 1976 or 1982. In 1988, the thirteen-year-olds performed just a bit better than their counterparts in the previous years. In 1976 and 1982, the average proficiency score was 49.1 and increased to 50.0 in 1988), While the average proficiency score of White thirteen-year-old students remained constant over the twelve-year period, "the proficiency of Black and Hispanic students at this age improved significantly" (National Assessment, 1990, p. 14). However, comparison of White-student scores to those of Black- and Hispanic-student average proficiency scores shows that there was, notwithstanding the gains made by Black- and Hispanic-students, an achievement gap at age thirteen and at age seventeen. For example, in 1988 at age thirteen the proficiency score for Whites was 51.2; for Blacks it was 45.7; and for Hispanics it was 45.5. In 1988, at age seventeen, the average proficiency score for Whites was 61.4; for Blacks it was 53.1; and for Hispanics it was 53.

Between 1976 and 1988, the scores of thirteen-year-olds who attended schools in advantaged urban area s declined "somewhat." In 1976, their proficiency score was 55.0 and 52.6 in 1988. The scores for thirteen-year-olds from disadvantaged urban areas "remained relatively constant." For seventeen-year-olds from advantaged areas, there was a significant decline in proficiency scores—from 66.1 to 62.3—between 1976 and 1988 just as there was a significant decline—from 56.3 to 50.0—between 1976 and 1988 in the proficiency scores for students from disadvantaged urban areas. Comparison of scores of students from advantaged urban areas to those from disadvantaged urban areas shows that there was an achievement gap between the two areas. For example, in 1988 the average proficiency score of thirteen-year-old students from advantaged urban areas was 52.6 and 43.8 for those from disadvantaged urban areas. In 1988, the average proficiency score for seventeen-year-olds was 62.3 and 50.0 for those from disadvantaged urban areas (National Assessment, 1990, p. 15).

The findings for fourth-, eighth, and twelfth-grade students basically mirrored those of the thirteen- and seventeen-year-olds. For example, ETS reported that: "At grade 4, there were large differences in the percentages of White students and either Black or Hispanic students who attained each level of civics proficiency." The civics achievement gap found at the fourth grade was not closed at the twelfth grade, but appears to have increased somewhat. The ETS summary reported that: "By the twelfth grade, the percentages of Black and Hispanic students who reached the uppermost levels of proficiency were far smaller than the percentage of White students who did" (National Assessment, 1990, p. 9).

It must be emphasized that there is no necessary cause-and-effect relationship between "students' proficiency and their demographic, school, or home characteristics or their instructional experiences." It must also be emphasized that while one group may not perform as well as another group, the reports of group performances "masks variations in the performance of individual students within any given subpopulation." Indeed, it is more than likely that in each group there were students who achieved at a high level and students who performed poorly (National Assessment, 1990, p. 41).

America 2000 and Goals 2000

Goals 2000: Educate America Act (Public Law 103-227), signed into law by President William J. Clinton on March 31, 1994, signified that the Congress and the president agreed that public education was on and indeed belonged on the national agenda. Its purpose, as expressed in Title I, was "to establish National Education Goals." The origins of Goals 2000 can be traced back to September 1989 when President George H. W. Bush met with forty-nine of the nation's governors on the campus of the University of Virginia for what was billed as a "bipartisan National Education Summit." Clinton, as governor of Arkansas, played an active and important role at the summit. He and President George H. W. Bush agreed on the need for national standards for public education, and they had the support of Albert Shanker, president of the American Federation of Teachers. At the Charlottesville Summit, the president and the governors agreed that it was time for the nation "to establish clear national [education] performance goals" that promised to make the nation "internationally competitive" (*America 2000*, 1991, p. 59). The "Summit" laid the foundation for Bush's *America 2000* that was released on April 18, 1991. In *America 2000*, it was reported that since 1980 "real spending" for education had increased by 33 percent but that "education trend lines" were "flat." Eight years after *A Nation at Risk* the nation still had not "turned things around in education" (*America 2000*, 1990, p. 15). Bush's *America 2000* argued that education was essential to the nation's standing in the international arena. He did not want American education to be second to that of any other nation:

> American's educational performance must be second to none in the 21st century. Education is central to our quality of life. It is at the heart of our economic strength and security, our creativity in the arts and letters, our invention in the sciences, and the perpetuation of our cultural values. Education is the key to America's international competiveness." (*America 2000*, 1991, p. 59)

America 2000 made it through the House of Representatives but died in the Senate. The Bush administration had planned to reintroduce *America 2000* to the Congress in its second term but there was no second term for the senior Bush. However, the effort Bush made cannot be considered a failure, for Clinton, as president, pushed forward with what was agreed upon at Charlottesville.

Goals 2000 served as continuation of the excellence and standards movements associated with *A Nation at Risk*, Bush's *America 2000*, and as a bridge between *A Nation at Risk* and No Child Left Behind. President George H. W. Bush's and President Clinton's responses to the 1989 National Governors' meetings on education show that interest in the nation's need for knowledgeable human capital overrode partisan politics. Each response (*America 2000* and Goals 2000) was an attempt to maintain the 1980s' calls for reform, standards, and excellence as well as to ensure equality of educational opportunity for at-risk students. The need to achieve equality of educational opportunity for all students and the need for knowledgeable human capital were becoming equally important, for increased academic achievement was needed so there would be a supply of knowledgeable human capital capable of making the nation competitive on the global marketplace. Bush and Clinton proposed adoption of voluntary national standards and testing of students in grades, 4, 8, and 12 in English, mathematics, science, and history.

Several of the goals declared in Title I of Goals 2000—NATIONAL EDUCATION GOALS—clearly indicate that the purpose of the legislation was to develop and to increase the supply of knowledgeable human capital, to promote interest in raising standards, especially in mathematics and science, and to improve the success and performance of students classified as belonging to a minority group.

Goal 2—SCHOOL COMPLETION—set a high school graduation rate of at least ninety percent by 2000. It specified that the nation needed to "dramatically reduce its school dropout rate" and declared that by 2000 75 percent of the dropouts "will successfully complete a high school degree or its equivalent." It further specified that "the gap in high school graduation rates between American students from minority backgrounds and their non-minority counterparts will be eliminated."

Goal 3—STUDENT ACHIEVEMENT AND CITIZENSHIP—focused on the competence that students in grades 4, 8, and 12 were to have "over challenging subject matter including English, mathematics, science, foreign languages, civics and government, economics, arts, history." In addition, schools were to ensure that students learned "to use their minds well" so they would be prepared for "responsible citizenship" and "productive employment in our Nation's modern economy." The objectives of GOAL 3 specified that the performance of all students was to "increase significantly in every quartile" and that "the distribution of minority students in each quartile will more closely reflect the student population as a whole." The sixth objective of GOAL 3 indicated an awareness and acceptance of the nation's cultural diversity. It specified that all students were to become "knowledgeable about the diverse cultural heritage of this Nation and about the world community."

GOAL 5—MATHEMATICS AND SCIENCE—asserted that: "By the year 2000, United States students will be first in the world in mathematics and science." Its objectives, included strengthening of mathematics and science education, "especially in the early grades"; increasing by 50 percent "the number of teachers with a substantive background in mathematics and science"; and increasing "significantly" the number of undergraduate and graduate students, "especially women and minorities who complete degrees in mathematics, science, and engineering." The emphasis of including more minorities and women in engineering was reminiscent of President Eisenhower's Committee on Education Beyond the High School that identified minorities and women as "underdeveloped areas of talent" in 1957 (President's Committee, 1957, p. 43) and *The Rockefeller Panel Report* that called for "Fuller Use of Underprivileged Minorities" and "Better Use of the Talents of Women" in 1958 (Report V, 1961, pp. 380–381).

The emphasis in Goals 2000 on the graduation rates and test scores of minorities shows that equality of educational opportunity was then defined neither in terms of access to equally supported schools nor in terms of desegregation but as achievement. As long as a consistent difference between majority graduation rates and test scores and minority graduation rates and test scores obtained, there was inequality.

By the 1980s, there was, especially with the advantage of hindsight, a clear movement to turn away from access and resource considerations when addressing equality of educational opportunity and a movement toward reforms that called for accountability, standards, and measures of academic achievement. That movement can be seen in reforms implemented in the several states in the 1980s, in *A Nation at Risk,* President Clinton's Goals 2000, and Clinton's "Educational Excellence for All Children" that was an attempt to "build on the standards and accountability framework that had been outlined—but never fully fleshed out in Goals 2000" (McGuinn, 2006, p. 137).

No Child Left Behind

At the beginning of the twenty-first century, Congress passed the No Child Left Behind Act (NCLB), another reauthorization of the 1965 Elementary and Secondary Education Act. It can be seen as having been designed to overcome what *The Coleman Report* documented in the mid-1960s: what is now commonly known as the "achievement gap," or what Christopher Jencks described as the "racial gap" (Jencks, 1966). Jencks claimed that the "racial gap" could not be overcome without massive federal interference in public education that many persisted in claiming was the prerogative of state and local authorities. Many now agree that No Child Left Behind has created federal interference and many have objected to that interference.

The interference about which many complain is NCLB's requirement that all states administer statewide tests in reading and in mathematics for grades three through eight. While some object to the testing requirements, there is also some controversy about the nature of the tests that are used. While NCLB allows states to develop their own tests provided they are aligned with state standards, others call for a universal national test, arguing that adoption of a national test would advance higher standards. Those who argue for a national test and the higher standards that would be advanced by a national test argue that their position would ensure that students would be thus better prepared to compete in the Global Economy. As long as each state has its own test, it becomes very difficult, if not impossible, to make comparisons between and among the states, for what constitutes academic proficiency varies from state to state. However, it should be noted that opposition to a federally required national test is very strong. In 1998 when President Clinton proposed only to make a national test available to the states, his proposal was defeated in the United States House of Representatives "by a bipartisan vote of 242–174" (Barone, 2008, p. 32). However, NCLB does seek to gather test results that allow comparisons between and among the states. Each state is required every other year to provide a sample of fourth- and eighth-grade students to participate in the National Assessment of Educational Progress (NAEP) in mathematics and reading. The states are required to provide test scores for individual students and report the scores by race, income, and other categories so that the progress and the achievement gaps of the subgroups can be ascertained.

No Child Left Behind was founded on the belief that schools can be effective. If there is any doubt about the relationship among educational reform, the need to achieve equality of educational opportunity, the need for knowledgeable human capital, and the national agenda, one only has to consider the emphasis that NCLB has placed on eliminating the achievement gap between students from the mainstream dominant classes and students from minority groups. That emphasis can be explained by considering estimates of the future racial-ethnic composition of the nation's population and by examining estimates of the future size and characteristics of the prime-age workforce (25 to 54 year olds). According to a report from the United States Census Bureau in 2006, between 2004 and 2005 the nation's population grew by 2.8 million, "and people of color accounted for 81 percent of that growth" (Jayakumar, 2008, p. 615).

Between 1980 and 2000 the prime-age workforce grew by 35.1 million. It is projected that between 2000 and 2020 the prime-age workforce will increase by only 3.1 million. In an era when success in the Global Economy depends on a highly educated workforce, the projections about the size and the characteristics of the prime-age workforce are significant. They explain why educators and politicians responded to the imperative of NCLB to eliminate the achievement gap between majority and minority students. Approximately 30 percent of the prime-age workforce between 2000 and 2020 is expected to come from a population that is classified as either African American or Hispanic students. That population most likely either will not enter college or if they enter, are not likely to be graduated (Kolb, 2006, pp. 54, 45). The reason that a significant number of African American and Hispanic students is not likely to enter college may be found in a study conducted by Johns Hopkins University that described approximately 1,700 regular or vocational high schools as "dropout factories." That study revealed that approximately 70 percent of students in the United States complete high school "on time." However, "for Hispanic and black students, the proportion drops to about half" (Zuckerbrod, 2007, p. 11).

Since 1972, the proportion of public school students classified as white has decreased significantly. In 1972, it was approximately 80 percent; in 2002 it was approximately 60 percent. The achievement gap, as measured by standardized tests, between African Americans and whites and between Hispanics and whites has been reduced "considerably," but it has not been eliminated. If those gaps and the gap between rich students and poor students are not eliminated, the nation's economy and its democracy will be "in danger" (Schrag, 2003, p. 245).

Another account suggests that college enrollment rates and graduation rates are not great enough to replace the college-educated workers who will retire in the coming decades. For example, it has been estimated that "the share of workers with at least some college will increase by only 3 percent between 2000 and 2020." Some projections show "that by 2012, we will have a surplus of more than three million workers with high-school degrees or less, and a shortage of about seven million workers with at least some college education" (Carnevale, 2006, p. B7). A report conducted with funds from the Lumina Foundation for Education projected that if current trends continue, by 2025 "the United States will have 15.6 million fewer bachelor's- and associate-degree holders than it needs to keep up with its top economic competitors." To reverse the trend, the nation needs its "annual degree production" to increase "by more than 37 percent." To achieve that increase it will be necessary to graduate "many more students who are members of minority groups, from low-income families, or beyond the traditional college age" (Schmidt, 2007, p. A25).

A study conducted by the Western Interstate Commission for Higher Education (WICHE) indicated that after 2008 when it is estimated that 3.34 million students will be graduated from high school the nation is expected to witness a slow decline in high school graduates until 2015. In 2015 "the rapidly growing Hispanic and Asian populations will push that number [3.34 million] to a new high." WICHE further projected that by 2022 nearly half of all public high-school graduates will be members of one of the nation's minority groups. About a fourth of the 2022 high-school graduates will be Hispanics. Many of those who go on to enroll in college will be first-generation students. A significant number of those who will then be enrolling in college will be the students "whom colleges have historically struggled to serve" (Ashburn, 2008, pp. 1A, 24A).

Another account reports that by 2020 the majority of public school students will be those who are "most educationally at-risk"—"Latinos and African Americans." In 2008 it was reported that while 75 percent of white students were likely to be awarded a regular high school diploma, only 50 percent for African American students were likely to be awarded the same kind of diploma. Enrollment in college and graduation from college is greater for white students than for African American students. When eighth graders are graduated from high school, 44 percent of African-American students enroll in college and 58 percent of white students enroll in college. Seventeen percent of the African-American students earn their bachelor's degree, and 35 percent of the white students earn their bachelor's degree (Rebell, 2008, p. 433).

Closing the achievement gap is a purpose endorsed by a majority of Americans. A survey in 2007 showed that the achievement gap was high on the national agenda. Sixty-seven percent of Americans believed it was "very important" to eliminate the achievement gap between white and minority (Black and Hispanic) students, and an additional 21 percent agreed that it was "somewhat important" to do so (Rose & Gallup, 2006, p. 46).

Coleman and No Child Left Behind

The minority groups Coleman identified—"Negroes, American Indians, Oriental Americans, Puerto Ricans living in the continental United States, Mexican Americans"—did not, as groups, perform as well in school, as the dominant group—"whites other than Mexican Americans and Puerto Ricans often called 'majority' or simply 'white'" (Coleman, 1966, p. iii). Coleman identified a major inequality—the lack of academic achievement among minority groups. Coleman was classifying Americans by race and ethnicity, but there were then no standard or official ways whereby Americans were so classified. In 1973, less than a decade after *The Coleman Report*, Casper Weinberger, then the Secretary of the United States Department of Health, Education, and Welfare, directed the Federal Interagency on Education "to develop consistent rules for classifying Americans by ethnicity and race." That led to the Office of Management and Budget's issuance of "Directive No. 15: Race and Ethnic Standards for Federal Statistics and Administrative Reporting" in 1977 (Lind, 1996, p. 119). While the groups

Coleman identified are not those—American Indian or Alaskan Native, Asian or Pacific Islander, Hispanic, White, Black—later officially designated by the Statistical Directive No. 15, there is a remarkable similarity.

No Child Left Behind can be interpreted as an attempt to remedy the inequalities—the achievement gap—documented in *The Coleman Report*. Coleman's identification of the lack of academic achievement among minority groups is addressed in No Child Left Behind. However, Coleman's argument that the social environment of many students contributes to unequal achievement and needed to be addressed was not accepted by No Child Left Behind. No Child Left Behind acknowledged that students identified as members of minority groups consistently perform less well in school than their counterparts from the dominant classes and stated as its purpose the elimination of the difference—the achievement gap—among the groups.

Once *The Coleman Report* was fully understood, those responsible for public education realized that they had to do more than simply find ways to "turn on" students so they would remain in school. Public education was soon to be accountable according to a new definition of equality of educational opportunity. As long as there was a high correlation between social class, race or ethnicity and poor school performance equality of educational opportunity did not obtain. Social class, race, and ethnicity were often once used to explain lack of academic achievement, but now educators were assigned the responsibility for finding ways to eliminate their predictive power.

Coleman urged that the teaching of reading and arithmetic—two subjects schools frequently failed to teach effectively to lower class children—"be opened up to entrepreneurs outside the school" (Coleman, 1967, p. 24). No Child Left Behind appears to have no explicit provision for employing entrepreneurs to teaching arithmetic and reading. However, districts receiving Title I funds are required to use reading programs that are supported by scientifically based research, and the current climate celebrates entrepreneurship and its employment by school districts.

No Child Left Behind rewards schools whose students achieve satisfactorily with additional resources and allows parents of "failing" schools to remove their children from failing schools. Schools that fail to show annual yearly progress for two consecutive years are required to offer students' parents the opportunity to transfer their children to another school provided that state law does not prohibit school choice. Those schools are then required to use up to 5 percent of their Title I funds to pay for students' transportation to another school. Schools that fail to demonstrate annual yearly progress for three consecutive years are allowed to use an additional 10 percent of their Title I funds for either transportation of students to another school or for supplemental instructional services—tutoring, after school classes, and summer school—for low achieving disadvantaged students. The provision of supplemental services is not limited to public schools. Faith-based organizations are allowed to provide such services. Districts with schools that fail to show annual yearly progress for four consecutive years are required to implement an improvement plan. Districts with schools that fail to show annual yearly progress for five consecutive years are required to develop and implement plans that would change how the school is administered, allow the state to take control of the school, hire a private entity to administer the school, restructure the school's staff, or convert it to a charter school. All failing schools are required to provide supplemental instructional services and to provide parents the opportunity to transfer their children to another school.

Coleman wanted to introduce competition between public schools and private contractors, and that was a way to achieve a measure of accountability. He claimed competition would either encourage or force schools to improve their programs. Schools would then presumably be able to adopt programs and innovations that worked in the private sector. No Child Left Behind also relies on competition. Schools are assigned grades, and thus competition is introduced not only between public schools and private schools but also between and among public schools within districts. Coleman advocated the introduction of choice through contracts with outside entrepreneurs. Contract schools would extend to public school users some choice comparable to that enjoyed by the wealthy and the middle classes who can afford to pay for education outside the public schools.

Coleman and Clark were not the only ones to urge that the public school monopoly be broken. Writing in 1967, as were Clark and Coleman, Fred M. Newman and Donald W. Oliver also expressed concern about the public school monopoly that "fundamentally altered the nature of childhood and adolescence in America" and "destroyed to a large extent the opportunities for random, exploratory work and play outside of a formal educational setting" (Newman & Oliver, 1967, p. 81).

No Child Left Behind can be seen as having been designed to resolve what is essentially a social justice issue—achieving equality of educational opportunity—as well as to address the nation's need for knowledgeable human capital. Indeed, there is some belief that pursuit of what No Child Left Behind requires has effectively "reshaped much of the conscious paradigm regarding American education research." According to James W. Guthrie, the federal "Institute of Education Sciences, along with the National Institute for Child Health and Development and the National Science Foundation, is supporting research initiatives using rigorous randomized experiments to evaluate educational products and practices" (Guthrie, 2005, p. 48). Such research, its adherents believe, will enable schools to eliminate what has come to be known as the "achievement gap."

No Child Left Behind may appear to have been designed to resolve what is essentially a social justice issue—the strong relationship that is consistently found between social class and school success—that has been an issue on the nation's agenda ever since, if not before, the appearance of the Elementary and Secondary Education Act in 1965 and *The Coleman Report* in 1966. No Child Left Behind requires that school districts disaggregate students' performances on standardized tests so it can be shown whether adequate yearly progress has been achieved by all students in the designated groups. That means districts must show the scores for each group: Students who are classified as belonging to one of the major racial ethnic groups; economically disadvantaged students; students with disabilities; and students whose English proficiency is limited. The desired political outcome—equal academic achievement between and among groups—determined how test results were to be analyzed and reported. Significant differences in scores between or among any of these designated groups are indicators of inequality of educational opportunity.

The Institute of Educational Sciences' commitment to scientifically based research merits consideration because it is an effective way to basically control the questions that researchers will investigate as they investigate ways to eliminate the achievement gap. As Catherine Cornbleth has observed: "The most harmful threat to the public interest stemming from the current push for scientific research in education and the scientific research procedures debate . . . lies in the diversion of attention and other resources from issues and research questions that simply do not fit the referred procedures and the "what works (best)" question" (Cornbleth, 2006, p. 202). The questions Cornbleth believes should be asked—questions about cultural influences and the effects of racism and sexism—are clearly not the questions that interest the Institute of Education Sciences. For example, the research priorities of the Department of Education published in the June 16, 2006 *Federal Register* concentrated "on studying conditions that are under the control of the education system: curriculum, instruction, assessment, the quality of teachers and administrators, accountability systems, and school choice" (Viadero, 2005, p. 30). Those priorities rest on the assumption that public schools can be effective and engage in the "rational exploitation of social talent." These priorities are clearly not those needed for a social-economic reconstruction of society.

The movement to support only education research that promises to demonstrate "what works," began with Congress' reauthorization of Title I of the Elementary and Secondary Education Act, now known as the No Child Left Behind Act. No Child Left Behind is founded on the belief that schools and teachers are solely responsible for student achievement. Now, however, educators wish to emphasize the social context. They are returning to what *The Coleman Report* demonstrated, that student achievement is more closely related to socioeconomic factors than to the quality of schools. In their discussion of the "relation of achievement to school characteristics," the authors of *Equality of Educational Opportunity* reported:

> The first finding is that the schools are remarkably similar in the way they relate to the achievement of their pupils when the socioeconomic background of the students is taken into account. It is known that socioeconomic factors bear a strong relation to academic achievement. When these factors are statistically controlled, however, it appears that differences between schools account for only a small fraction of differences in pupil achievement. (Coleman, 1966, pp. 20–21)

Those who want to place all responsibility for student achievement on schools and teachers and ignore what *Equality of Educational Opportunity* revealed only need to return to accountability, the technological perspective, and what came to be known as the process-product research or continue to look for cause-and-effect relationships so they can tell teachers "what works." They do indeed want to ignore that "studies of school practices have consistently discovered powerful effects of family background on educational outcomes, much more powerful than the influence of schooling resources" (Tate, 2006, p. 251). They may also ignore Coleman's strong recommendation that public schools exert more and more effective influence over children's lives.

Some now maintain that the achievement gap can only be eliminated by a better understanding of how the social context in which a student is nurtured and educated and not by continuing the test-based accountability required by No Child Left Behind. American students' performance in mathematics and science on tests administered by the Program in International Student Assessment (PISA) in 2006 showed a decline over a three-year period. Among the top forty countries, the United States ranked thirty-fifth in mathematics and thirty-first in science (Darling-Hammond & McCloskey, 2008, p. 263). NCLB had no immediate effect.

Notes

1. Nearly all lists of the 1980s' "national reports" include *A Nation at Risk* and the following: Ernest L. Boyer. *High School: A Report on Secondary Education in America* (New York: Harper & Row, 1983); College Board. *Academic Preparation for College: What Students Need to Know and Be Able to Do* (New York: College Entrance Examination Board, 1983); Philip A. Cusick. *The Egalitarian Ideal and the American High School* (New York: Longman, 1983); Linda Darling-Hammond. *Beyond the Commission Reports: The Coming Crisis in Teaching* (Washington, D. C,: Rand, 1984); John I. Goodlad. *A Place Called School: Prospects for the Future* (New York: McGraw-Hill, 1984); Sara Lawrence Lightfoot. *The Good High School: Portraits of Character and Culture* (New York: Basic Books, 1983); The National Science Board's Commission on Precollege Education in Mathematics, Science, and Technology. *Educating Americans for the Twenty-First Century* (Washington, D. C.: National Science Board, 1983); Task Force on Education for Economic Growth. *Action for Excellence: A Comprehensive Plan to Improve Our Nation's Schools* (Washington, D. C.: Education Commission of the States, 1983); Task Force on Federal Elementary and Secondary Education Policy. *Making the Grade* (New York: The Twentieth Century Fund, 1983); and Theodore Sizer. *Horace's Compromise: The Dilemma of the American High School* (Boston: Houghton Mifflin, 1984). The following are sometimes included in lists of "national reports:" Mortimer Adler. *The Paideia Proposal: An Educational Manifesto* (New York: Macmillan, 1982) and *Paideia Problems and Possibilities: A Consideration of Questions Raised by the Paideia Proposal* (New York: Macmillan, 1983).
2. *Making the Grade* reprinted in *Education Week*, Vol. 2 (May 11, 1983), p. 14.
3. The Advisory Council was chaired by David A. Hamburg, President of Carnegie Corporation.
4. Other members of the Task Force included: Alan K. Campbell, Vice-Chairman of the Board and Executive Vice-President of ARA Services; Mary Hatwood Futrell, President, National Education Association; John W. Gardner; Fred M. Hechinger, President, The New York Times Company Foundation; Bill Honig, Superintendent of Public Instruction, State of California; James B. Hunt, Attorney, Poyner & Spruill; Vera Katz, Speaker of the Oregon House of Representatives; Thomas H. Kean, Governor of New Jersey; Judith Lanier, Dean, College of Education, Michigan State University; Arturo Madrid, President, The Tomas Rivera Center; Shirley M. Malcom, Program Head, Office of Opportunities in Science, American Association for the Advancement of Science; Ruth E. Randall, Commissioner of Education, State of Minnesota; and Albert Shanker, President, American Federation of Teachers.

References

America 2000: An education strategy. (1991). Washington, DC: U.S. Government Printing Office.

Angus, D. L., & Mirel, J. E. (1999). *The failed promise of the American high school, 1890–1995.* New York: Teachers College.

Ashburn, E. (2008, March 38). Student pool is expected to dip and diversify. *The Chronicle of Higher Education, LIV*(29).

Barone, C. (2008, November 19). Could 'open source' testing help resolve the testing impasse? *Education Week, 28*(13).

Barron, C. K. (1951, May). Points of resistance to curriculum change. *Progressive Education, 28*(7).

Bell, B. I. (1949). *Crisis in education: A challenge to American complacency.* New York: McGraw-Hill.

Bell-Rose, S., & Payzant, T. W. (2008, August 13). The case for entrepreneurship education. *Education Week, 27*(45).

Bestor, A. E. (1953). *Educational wastelands: The retreat from learning in our public schools.* Urbana: University of Illinois Press.

Bestor, A. E. (1956). *The restoration of learning.* New York: Alfred A. Knopf.

Board of Education of St. Louis. (1936). *Eighty-Second Annual Report.*

Borstelmann, T. (2001). *The cold war and the color line: American race relations in the global arena.* Cambridge, MA: Harvard University Press.

Boyer, E. L. (1991). Elementary and secondary education. In D. W. Hornbeck & L. M. Salamon (Eds.), *Human capital and America's Future: An economic strategy for the '90s.* Baltimore, MD: The Johns Hopkins University Press.

Brainard, J. (2007a, August 10). Teaching math and science may get boost from congress. *The Chronicle of Higher Education, LIII*(49).

Equality of Educational Opportunity and Knowledgeable Human Capital, pages 153–162

Brainard, J. (2007b, December 21). Texas offers a model for training math and science teachers. *The Chronicle of Higher Education, LIV*(17).

Broudy, H. S., Smith, B. O., & Burnett, J. R. (1964). *Democracy and excellence in secondary education.* Chicago: Rand McNally.

Brown v. Board of Education, 349. U.S. 294. (1974). In S. Cohen (Ed.), *Education in the United States: A documentary history.* New York: Random House.

Brown, M. (2008, February 23). High school report card is grim. *Tampa Tribune.*

Bruner, J. S. (1961). *The process of education.* Cambridge, MA: Harvard University Press.

Bruner, J. S. (1977). *The process of education* reconsidered. In G. Hass (Ed.), *Curriculum planning: A new approach.* Boston: Allyn & Bacon.

Brzezinski, Z. (1970). *Between two ages: America's role in the technetronic era.* New York: Viking Press.

Burgess, C., & Borrowman, M. L. (1969). *What doctrines to embrace: Studies in the history of education.* Glenview, IL: Scott, Foresman and Co.

Bush, V. (1949). *Modern arms and free men: A discussion of the role of science in preserving democracy.* New York: Simon and Schuster.

Bushaw, W. J., & Gallup, A. M. (2008, September). The 40th annual Phi Delta Kappa/Gallup poll of the public's attitudes toward the public schools. *Phi Delta Kappan. 90*(1).

The Carnegie Forum on Education and the Economy's Task Force on Teaching as a Profession. (1986). *A nation prepared: Teachers for the 21st century.* New York: The Carnegie Corporation of New York.

Carnevale, A. O. (2006, September 22). Discounting education's value. *The Chronicle of Higher Education,* Section B (*The Chronicle Review*), *LIII*(5).

Cavanagh, S. (2008, April 2). Essential qualities of math teaching remain unknown. *Education Week, 27*(31).

Cavanagh, S. (2007a, October 10). Federal rule yields hope for science. *Education Week, 27*(7).

Cavanagh, S. (2007b, December 12). Poverty's effect on U.S. scores than for other nations. *Education Week, 27*(15).

Cavanagh, S. (2007c, June 12). What kind of math matters? *Education Week, 26*(40).

Cavanagh, S. (2009, January 21). Standards help Minn[esota] view with top nations. *Education Week, 28*(18).

Christian, D., Pufahl, I., & Rhodes, N. C. (2005, November). Fostering foreign language proficiency: What the U.S. can learn from other countries. *Phi Delta Kappan, 87*(3).

Clark, D. L., Astuto, T. A., & Rooney, P. M. (1983, November). The changing structure of federal education policy in the 1980s. *Phi Delta Kappan, 65*(3).

Clark, K. (1968, Winter). Alternative public school systems. *Harvard Educational Review, 38*(1).

Clowse, B. B. (1981). *Brainpower for the cold war: The Sputnik Crisis and the National Defense Education Act of 1958.* Westport, CT: Greenwood Press.

Cohen, D. K., & Barnes, C. A. (1999). Research and the purposes of education. In E. C. Lagemann & L. S. Shulman (Eds.), *Issues in education research: Problems and possibilities.* San Francisco: Josey-Bass.

Cohen, D. K., & Garet, M. S. (1975, February). Reforming educational policy with applied social research. *Harvard Educational Review, 45*(1).

Cohen, S. (Ed.). (1975). *Education in the United States: A documentary history* (Vol. 5). New York: Random House.

Coleman, J. S. (1968, Winter). The concept of equality of educational opportunity. *Harvard Educational Review, 38*(1).

Coleman, J. S. (1967, Fall). Toward open schools. *The Public Interest,* (9).

Coleman, J. S., Campbell, E. Q., Hobson, C. J., McPartland, J., Mood, A. M., Weinfeld, F. D., & York, R. L. (1966). *Equality of educational opportunity.* Washington, DC: U.S. Government Printing Office.

Commission on the Reorganization of Secondary Education. (1918). *Cardinal principles of secondary education.* United States Bureau of Education. Washington, DC: U.S. Government Printing Office.

The Committee for The White House Conference on Education. (1956, April). *A report to the President.* Washington, DC: U.S. Government Printing Office.

Conant, J. B. (1948). *Education in divided world: The function of the public schools in our unique society.* Cambridge, MA: Harvard University Press.

Conant, J. B. (1959a). *The American high school today: A first report to interested citizens.* New York: McGraw-Hill.

Conant, J. B. (1959b). *The child, the parent, and the state.* Cambridge, MA: Harvard University Press.

Conant, J. B. (1960). *A memorandum to school boards: Recommendations for education in the junior high school years.* Princeton, NJ: Educational Testing Service.

Conant, J. B. (1961). *Slums and suburbs.* New York: McGraw-Hill.

Cornbleth, C. (2006). Curriculum and students: Diverting the public interest. In G. Ladson-Billings & W. F. Tate (Eds.), *Education research in the public interest: Social justice, action, and policy.* New York: Teachers College Press.

Cornog. W. H. (1959, October 25). *The Chicago Sunday Tribune.*

Costrell, R. M. (2007). The winning defense in Massachusetts. In M. R. West & P. E. Peterson (Eds.), *School money trails: The legal pursuit of educational adequacy.* Washington, DC: The Brookings Institution.

Cremin, L. A. (1962). *The transformation of the school: Progressivism in American education, 1876–1957.* New York: Alfred A. Knopf.

Cross, K. P. (1984, November). The rising tide of school reform reports. *Phi Delta Kappan, 66*(3).

Currence, C. (1985, October 7). Reforms could increase dropouts, dilute curriculum, study says. *Education Week, 5.*

Darling-Hammond, L. (1984, July). *Beyond the commission reports: The coming crisis in teaching.* Santa Monica CA: Rand Corporation.

Darling-Hammond, L. (2007, December 21). We need to invest in math and science teachers. *The Chronicle of Higher Education, LIV*(17).

Darling-Hammond, L., & McCloskey, L. (2008, December). Assessment for learning around the world: What would it mean to be internationally competitive? *Phi Delta Kappan. 90*(4).

Davies, G. (2007). *See government grow: Education politics from Johnson to Reagan.* Lawrence: University Press of Kansas.

Davis, A. (1951, May). Education for the conservation of human resources. *Progressive Education, 27*(7).

Division of International Education, International Educational Relations Branch, U.S. Office of Education. (1957). Bulletin 1957, No. 14. *Education in the USSR.* Washington, DC.

Dudziak, M. L. (2000). *Cold war civil rights: Race and the image of American democracy.* Princeton, NJ: Princeton University Press.

Educational Policies Commission. (1956). *Manpower and education.* Washington, DC: National Education Association.

Educators: Pleas for better math and U.S. billions. (1958, January 13). *Life, 44*(2).

Embree, E. R. (1942). *The American Negro: A bandbook.* New York: The John Day Co.

Field, K. (2008, September 5). Congress shows colleges they're not off the hook on accountability. *The Chronicle of Higher Education, LV*(2).

Fine, B. (1945). *Democratic education.* New York: Thomas Y. Crowell.

Fiske, E. B. (1983, April 10). Students gain in basic skills but high school scores fall. *The New York Times.*

The Ford Foundation. (1972). A *foundation goes to school: The Ford Foundation comprehensive school improvement program, 1960–1970.* New York: The Foundation.

Foreign language study booming. (2007, November 14). *The Tampa Tribune.*

Gage, N. (Ed.). (1963). *Handbook of research on teaching.* Chicago: Rand McNally.

Ginsberg, E. (1975). *The manpower connection: Education and work.* New York: Columbia University Press.

Goldberg, M., & Harvey, J. (1983, September). A nation at risk: The report of the National Commission on Excellence in Education. *Phi Delta Kappan, 65.*

Goodman, P. (1960, December 25). *New York Herald Tribune Lively Arts.*

Graham, H. D. (1990). *The civil rights era: Origins and development of national policy, 1960–1972.* New York: Oxford University Press.

Graubard, A. (1972, August). The free school movement. *Harvard Educational Review, 42*(3).

Green, A. (1983, May 11). Schools, businesses should be 'partners' in economic push. *Education Week, 2.*

Greenberg, J. (1994.) *Crusaders in the courts: How a dedicated band of lawyers fought for the civil rights revolution.* New York: Basic Books.

Guthrie, J. W. (2005, May 4). For want of a nail.... *Education Week, 24*(34).

Halliday, F. (2001). Cold war. In J. Krieger (Ed.), *The Oxford companion to the politics of the world* (2nd ed.) New York: Oxford University Press.

Harrington, M. (1961). *The other America.* New York: Macmillan.

Hechinger, F. M. (1959, February 15). *The New York Times.*

Help! Teacher can't teach! (1980, June 16). *Time.*

Higher education for democracy: A report of the President's commission on higher education. (1947). New York: Harper & Brothers.

Hoff, D. (2007, September). Law's timeline on proficiency under debate. *Education Week, 27*(5).

Hoff, D. J., & Cavanagh, S. (2007, May 2). Math-science bills advance in congress. *Education Week, 26*(35).

Hofstadter, R. (1963). *Anti-Intellectualism in American life.* New York: Alfred A. Knopf.

Honig, B. (1985, June). The educational excellence movement: Now comes the hard part. *Phi Delta Kappan, 66.*

Hornbeck, D. W., & Salamon, L. M. (Eds.). (1991). *Human capital and America's future.* Baltimore, MD: Johns Hopkins University Press.

House, E. R. (1981). Three perspectives on innovation: Technological, political and cultural. In R. Lehming & M. Kane (Eds.), *Improving schools: Using what we know.* Beverly Hills, CA: Sage.

How good is your school? *Life*'s test will tell you. (1950, October 16). *Life, 29*(16).

How U.S. wastes its gifted children. (1958, April 7). *Life, 44*(14).

Howe II, H. (1983, November). Education moves to center state: An overview of recent studies. *Phi Delta Kappan, 65*(3).

Hunt, H. (1956, May). Educational research and national educational policy. *Journal of Educational Research, XLIX*(9).

Hunt, M. H. (2007). *The American ascendancy: How the United States gained and wielded global dominance.* Chapel Hill: University of North Carolina Press.

Janowitz, M. (1969). *Institution building in urban education.* New York: Russell Sage Foundation.

Jayakumar, U. M. (2008, Winter). Can higher education meet the needs of an increasingly diverse and global society? Campus diversity and cross-cultural workforce competencies. *Harvard Educational Review, 78*(4).

Jefferson, T. (1961). A bill for the more general diffusion of knowledge. In G. C. Lee (Ed.), *Crusade against ignorance: Thomas Jefferson on education.* New York: Teachers College Press.

Jencks, C. (1966, October). Education: The racial gap. *New Republic, 155*(4).

Jencks, C. (1959, November 9). *The New Republic, 141*(23).

Jenkins, W. (Ed.). (1961). *The nature of knowledge: Implications for the education of teachers.* Milwaukee: University of Wisconsin-Milwaukee.

Jennings, F. G. (1960, October 15). A friend of the learning child. *Saturday Review, 43*(94).

Jennings, J. F. (1987, October). The Sputnik of the eighties. *Phi Delta Kappan, 69*(2).

Kelly, A. E. (2008, December). Reflections on the National Mathematics Advisory Panel final report. *Educational Researcher, 37*(9).

Kerlinger, F. N. (Ed.). (1973). *Review of research in education I.* Itasca, IL: F. E. Peacock Publishers.

Kerr, C. (1963). *The uses of the university.* New York: Harper and Row.

Kevles, D. J. (1978). *The physicists: The history of a scientific community in modern America.* New York: Alfred A. Knopf.

Kirst, M. W. (1981, Summer). Loss of support for public secondary schools: Some causes and solutions. *Daedalus.*

Kolb, C. E. M. (2006, July 12). The cracks in our education pipeline. *Education Week, 25*(42).

Krug, E. A. (1966). *Salient dates in American education.* New York: Harper & Row.

Lagemann, E. C., & Shulman, L. S. (Eds.). (1999). *Issues in education: Problems and possibilities.* San Francisco: Josey-Bass.

Laosa, L. M. (1984). Social policies toward children of diverse ethnic, racial, and language groups in the United States. In H. W. Stevenson & A. E. Siegel (Eds.), *Child development research and social policy.* Chicago: University of Chicago Press.

Lawson, S. F. (Ed.). (2004). *To secure these rights: The report of the president's committee on civil rights.* Boston: Bedford/St. Martins.

Lee, G. C. (Ed.). (1961). *Crusade against ignorance: Thomas Jefferson on education.* New York: Teachers College Press.

Lehming, R., & Kane, M. (Eds.). (1981). *Improving schools: Using what we know.* Beverly Hills, CA: Sage.

Levin, H. M. (1982, November). Federal grants and educational equity. *Harvard Educational Review, 52*(4).

Levine, E. I., & Wexler, E. M. (1981). *PL 94-142: an Act of Congress.* New York: Macmillan.

Lind, M. (1996). *The next American generation: The new nationalism and the fourth American generation.* New York: Free Press.

Lynd, A. (1950). *Quackery in the public schools.* Boston: Little, Brown.

Maeroff, G. I. (1982). *Don't blame the kids: The trouble with America's schools.* New York: McGraw-Hill.

Maeroff, G. I. (1983, June 26). Teachers unions are courted and castigated. *The New York Times.*

Marland, Jr., S. P. (1972, February). Accountability in education. *Teachers College Record, 73.*

Martin, D. T., Overholt, G., & Urban, W. J. (1976). *Accountability in American education.* Princeton, NJ: Princeton Book Co.

McGrath, J. E. (1953, May). Foreign language instruction in American schools. *Progressive Education, 30*(7).

McGuinn, P. J. (2006). *No child left behind and the transformation of federal education policy, 1965–2005.* Lawrences: University Press of Kansas.

Monastersky, R. (2007, September 21). The real science crisis: Bleak prospects for young researchers. *The Chronicle of Higher Education, LIV*(4).

Mosteller, F., & Moynihan, D. P. (Eds.). (1972). *On equality of educational opportunity.* New York: Vintage Books.

Myrdal, G. (1962). *An American dilemma: The Negro problem and American democracy* (20th anniversary ed.). New York: Harper and Row.

Nash, R. J., & Agne, R. M. (1972, February). The ethos of accountability–A critique. *Teachers College Record, 73.*

The National Assessment of Educational Progress. (1990, April). *The civics report card.* Princeton, NJ: Educational Testing Service.

National Association of School Principals. (1956). *The White House Conference on Education, November 28–December 1, 1955, Washington DC.* Downloaded from http://bul.sagepub.com at University of South Florida on February 26, 2007.

National Center for Education Statistics, Institute of Education Sciences. (2006). *The Condition of Education 2006.* Washington, DC: U.S. Department of Education.

National Commission on Excellence in Education. (1983). *A nation at risk: The imperative for educational reform.* Washington, DC: Government Printing Office., 1983.

National Manpower Council. (1960). *Education and manpower.* New York: Columbia University Press.

National Science Foundation and the Department of Education. (1980). *Science and engineering education for the 1980s and beyond.* Washington, DC: U.S. Government Printing Office.

Neckerman, K. M. (2007). *Schools betrayed: Roots of failure in inner-city education.* Chicago: University of Chicago Press.

Newman, F. M., & Oliver, D. W. (1967, Winter). Education and community. *Harvard Educational Review, 37.*

Office of Education. (n.d.). *Life adjustment education for every youth.* Washington, DC: Government Printing Offic.

Perrone, V., & Strandberg, W. (1972, February). A perspective on accountability. *Teachers College Record, 73.*

Phenix, P. H. (1964). *Realms of meaning: A philosophy of the curriculum for general education.* New York: McGraw-Hill.

Pipho, C. (1982, September). States move to reestablish academic standards in public schools and colleges. *Phi Delta Kappan, 64.*

Powell, A. G. (1980). *The uncertain profession: Harvard and the search for educational authority.* Cambridge, MA: Harvard University Press.

Pratt, H. (2007, October 10). Science education's overlooked ingredient. *Education Week, 27*(7).

The President's Committee on Education Beyond the High School. (1957). *Second report to the president.* Washington, DC: U.S. Government Printing Office.

Prospect for America: The Rockefeller Panel Reports. (1961). Garden City, New York: Doubleday.

Ravitch, D. (1981, April 18). The schools we deserve. *The New Republic.*

Ravitch, D. (1983). *The troubled crusade: American education, 1945–1980.* New York: Basic Books.

Rebell, M. (2008, February). Equal opportunity and the courts. *Phi Delta Kappan, 89*(6).

Renegotiating society's contract with the public schools: The National Commission on secondary education for Hispanics and the National Board of Inquiry into schools. (1985, Fall/Winter). *Carnegie Quarterly, 29, 30.*

Report V. (1961). The pursuit of excellence: Education and the future of America. In *Prospects for America: The Rockefeller panel reports.* Garden City, NY: Doubleday.

Reuben, J., & Perkins, L. (2007, August). Introduction: Commemorating the sixtieth anniversary of the President's Commission Report, *Higher education for democracy. History of Education Quarterly, 47*(3).

Richardson, T. R., & Johanningmeier, E. V. (2003). *Race, ethnicity, and education: What is taught in schools.* Greenwich, CT: Information Age.

Robinson, D. W. (1973, March). Alternative schools: Do they promise reform?" *Phi Delta Kappan, 54*(7).

Rose, L. C., & Gallup, A. M. (2006, September). The 38th annual Phil Delta Kappan/Gallup poll of the public's attitudes toward the public schoosl. *Phi Delta Kappan, 88*(1).

Rosenberg, J. M. (1966). *Automation, manpower, and education.* New York: Random House.

Salamon, L. M. (1991). Overview: Why human capital? Why now? In D. W. Hornbeck & L. M. Salamon (Eds.), *Human capital and America's future.* Baltimore, MD: Johns Hopkins University Press.

Schmidt, P. (2007, March 16). America falls behind in degree attainment, report warns. *The Chronicle of Higher Education, LIII*(28).

The scholars look at the schools: A report of the disciplines seminar. (1962). Washington, DC: The National Education Association.

Schrag, P. (2003). *Final test: The battle for adequacy in America's schools.* New York: The New Press.

Scott, W. C., & Hill, C. M. (Eds.). (1954). *Public education under criticism.* Englewood Cliffs, NJ: Prentice-Hall.

Sevilla, E. (2008, March 17). Why 'second-best' won't doom college-bound kids. *USA Today.*

Smith, M. (1949). *And madly teach: A layman looks at public school education.* Chicago: Henry Regnery.

Smith, V. H. (1973, March). Options in public education: The quiet revolution. *Phi Delta Kappan, 54*(7).

Spady, W. G. (1973). The impact of school resources on students. In F. N. Kerlinger (Ed.), *Review of research in education I.* Itasca, IL: F. E. Peacock Publishers.

Stack, J. H. (1960, January 25). *Chemical and Engineering News, 38*(80).

Stedman, L. C., & Smith, M. S. (1983, Fall). Recent reform proposals for American education. *Contemporary Education Review, 2.*

Stevenson, H. W., & Siegel, A. E. (Eds.). (1984). *Child development research and social policy.* Chicago: University of Chicago Press.

Strickland, C. (1985, Spring). Sputnik reform revisited. *Educational Studies, 16.*

Sullivan, G. J. (1961, June 26). The natural approach to learning. *Commonweal, 74*(334).

Sundquist, J. L. (1968). *Politics and policy The Eisenhower, Kennedy, and Johnson years.* Washington, DC: The Brookings Institution.

Swanson, C. B. (2007, June 12). Learning and earning. *Education Week, 26*(40).

Task Force for Economic Growth. (1983). *Action for excellence: A comprehensive plan to improve our nation's schools.* Washington, DC: Education Commission of the States.

Tate, W. F. (2006). In the public interest. In G. Ladson-Billings & W. F. Tate (Eds.), *Education research in the public interest: Social justice, action, and policy.* New York: Teachers College Press.

Theobald, R. (1962). *The challenge of abundance.* New York: A Mentor Book.

Tumin, M. M., & Bressler, M. (1966). *Conference on "Quality and equality in education.* Cooperative Research Project No. F-048. Princeton, NJ.

U.S. betters math scores. (2008, December 10). *The Tampa Tribune.*

U.S. Office of Education, Division of International Education, International Educational Relations Branch. (1957). *Education in the USSR.* Washington, DC: U.S. Government Printing Office.

Viadero, D. (2008, April 16). Black-white gap widens faster for high achievers. *Education Week, 27*(33).

Viadero, D. (2005, July 13). Learning by at-risk students tops list of proposed research priorities. *Education Week, 24*(41).

Waller, W. (1943, September). The family and other institutions. *The Annals of the American Academy of Political Science: The American Family in World War II* (Vol. 229). Washington, DC: The American Academy of Political and Social Science.

Warner, W. L., Havighurst, R. J., & Loeb, M. B. (1944). *Who shall be educated?* New York: Harper and Brothers.

Watson. P. (2002). *The modern mind: An intellectual history of the 20th century.* New York: Harper Collins.

Weise, E. (2007, November 20). As China booms, so does Mandarin in U.S. schools. *USA Today.*

West, M. R., & Peterson, P. E. (Eds.). *School money trials: The legal pursuit of educational adequacy*. Washington, DC: The Brookings Institution.

What U.S. thinks about its schools: Roper survey finds both complacency and dissatisfaction. (1950, October 16). *Life, 29*(16).

Zuckerbrod, N. (2007, November 2). Report criticizes U.S. high schools as 'dropout factories'. *The Tampa Tribune.*

Index

A

Equality of Educational Opportunity and Knowledgeable Human Capital, pages 163–175

B

C

F

G

H

N

P

Q

R

S

T

U

9 781607 522317

Printed and bound by CPI Group (UK) Ltd, Croydon, CR0 4YY

15/09/2026

14962367-0008